God's Firestarters

Preparing Our Families for Coming Revivals

by Rev. Dr. Ed and Janice Hird

From the Book Series
Strengthening a New Generation of Healthy Leaders

HISPUBLISHING
GROUP

www.hispubg.com
A division of HISpecialists, llc

I encourage you to not only read this *God's Firestarter* book, but even other books written by the same authors. Just one example, "Celebrating the differences" as enrichment instead of taking them as issues. I bless you, Ed+ and Janice, as you use your gift of writing.

—The Most Rev Kolini Musaba Emmanuel (Rtd. Archbishop of Rwanda)

When the sun's light hits a gem at just the right angle, it catches our eye, it sparkles, it draws us closer. Ed and Janice Hird have caught these gems of the Faith in just the right perspective, heartfelt relationships with spouse and God, for them to shine for us and fill our hearts with hope and hopefully, close enough for fire.

—The Right Rev'd Carl Buffington, New Covenant Church, Winter Spring, Florida, Anglican Mission International

This is a book this world desperately needs! As it says in the book of Jude verse 3, "I felt compelled to write and urge you to contend for the faith that was once for all entrusted to God's holy people." Thank you, Dr. Ed and Janice for giving your readers to know how the Holy Spirit kindled the fire of those holy people in the past several hundred years through their witness of their family, especially relationships of husbands and wives in the twenty chapters to set on fire so many people to live for Jesus that He is our Lord and King. And, most important, to set us on FIRE!

—Rt. Rev. Dr. Silas Ng (Chief Bishop, Anglican Mission in Canada)

Ed and Janice Hird create a spirit of excitement and expectancy in "God's Firestarters" with their realistic portrayal of giants who moved the church in the Spirit. Revival through fiery preaching, yes, Holy Spirit anointing, yes, but also with roots in family life, marriage tensions, quirks and tempers, faith, much prayer, service, learning, study, holy and sacrificial living. The united picture gives us a sense of what it would take to know God's visitation very realistically sparked among us today.

—Bishop Alf Cooper (Chile)

I have known Dr Ed Hird since 1992. His life and ministry have been dedicated to Jesus, the renewal of the Church, and the strengthening of the family. In this masterpiece, he and Janice once again point us in the direction of the necessity and means of renewal and awakening through sharing the stories of men and women who came face to face WITH God and hence experienced his reviving fire. This is a powerful book. Read it and you will be renewed by the Holy Spirit as you pay heed to his voice.

—The Rt Rev'd Dr Felix Orji, Diocesan Bishop Anglican Diocese of the West. Coordinating Bishop of CONNAM.

Spiritual Fire-starters are people lovers, risk takers, tireless workers and servant leaders who are characterized by wet eyes, bent knees and a humble spirit crying for revival. This is what this book is all about, and the anointing Rev Dr Ed & Janice Hird carry. I highly endorse this book.

—The Rev Dr Medad Birungi Zinomuhangi, PhD
Founder & President of World Shine Ministries, Uganda

As always, you have outdone yourself, giving us hope that God will raise up new fire-starters in our day to push back the flames of temptation and plagues of corruption. I would highly recommend that everyone pick up a copy of this book and be inspired by the lives of ordinary people who were filled with their extraordinary God and accomplished huge things. You have always acted with a prophetic calling to awaken people to what is possible with God working in and through them. This is just another book in your storied career that will ignite numerous people to trust God for bigger things than they were prepared for. When we forget the past, we are weaker in the present and nonexistent in the future.

—Dr. Gil Stieglitz, author of *Building a Ridiculously
Great Marriage and Wise Parenting*

Rarely does historical research, literary talent, common sense and spiritual insight come together to ignite a fire in my head and my heart at the same time. However, this was the case as I read this clear, comprehensible manuscript from Ed and Janice Hird. I will read it with my wife and with my grandchildren because it will spark conversations that cannot be found any other way. Please do not miss the opportunity to use this book to increase the number of God's Firestarters in your family and in our world today.

—Rev. Tom Albin, Executive Director, United Christian Ashrams (UCA) and
President of the National Association of United Methodist Evangelists (NAUME)

God's Firestarters is a great book and an inspiration to let us know that even in pain and suffering, God and the people of God always prevail. These great men and women mentioned in the Bible, like the Apostle Paul, did not have it easy, but God used their trials to impact the world.

—Wesley Hunter, Chair, United Christian Ashram International Council

God's Firestarters is a book for all time and especially for our time. Ed and Janice Hird have written the stories of 20 "on-fire" leaders who followed Christ and whose examples we need today. Allow these inspiring voices to light your fire for God's next great awakening!

—Tom Nisbett, Ph.D., CFRE
ExploreX and Orchard Ministries
Ozark Highlands.

A captivating gift of story-telling wrapped in historical exploration and riveting case-studies that brings out multiple elixirs for revival today and ecclesial empowerment.

—Dr. Leonard Sweet, best-selling author (*Rings of Fire*), professor (George Fox University, Evangelical Seminary, Tabor College), and founder of The Salish Sea Press and preachthestory.com

Having known Ed Hird for decades, I have always admired his passion for the Lord, and authentic honour, for those of generations past who have impacted history through their consecration hearts and laid down lives. This book reflects, with vigor, that passion and is nothing short of a treasure chest of revelation and inspiration. Like **master excavators**, Rev. Ed and Janice Hird have chiseled out of the rock of history gems that reveal what God can do with humble, devoted, individuals — many of whom are profoundly relatable. These stories both inspire and invite each one of us to step into the storyline of history in a way that will echo through eternity, by God's grace. I believe these pages will leave every open heart aflame with fresh fire and passion!"

— Faytene Grasseschi, 4 MY Canada / V-Kol Media / Faytene TV

God's Firestarters is like an evangelical box of matches where any chapter could flare up with inspiration and start a fire in the heart of the reader. Perhaps this book should carry a disclaimer, warning the reader they could develop a severe case of enthusiasm for missions! The Hirds have done a great service in bringing such a diverse cast of heroes together in one volume. The book will take you on a 500-year journey from Katharina Luther to J I Packer and at the end you will be hungry for more.

— Pastor David G Carson, Intercessors For Canada

Dr. Ed and Janice Hird have brought to life their stories masterfully sharing about their personal histories filled with the accounts of their triumphs and troubles, their strengths and their weaknesses but most significantly; the joys and sorrows they experienced pursuing their highest convictions and calling despite the opposition and persecution.

God's Firestarters reminds us again through their stories unequivocally; that God can and will use any vessel regardless of their flaws and failures to ignite and set ablaze a city, a region and a nation for God. Thank you, Ed and Janice, for an amazing literary work that will surely impact every reader."

—Rev. Giulio Lorefice Gabeli
Overseer for Western Canada, Canadian Assemblies of God

Many have prayed for true revival by the Spirit of God. Few recognize the vital role that family plays in ushering in a move of God. Ed and Janice Hird understand. They've crafted a wealth of biographical research that not only brings pioneers of the faith to life, but also proves that family isn't an afterthought in God's plan. Instead, families are essential to bring forth true revival that endures for the generations. Enjoy this anthology of relational wisdom and receive His heart for what is treasure, indeed - our families.

—Laurel Thomas, Novelist and founder of Write Your Heart Out!

There is something of the rebel in Ed and Janice Hird. Their ability, and fortitude, to stand against the tide of liberalism has caused irrevocable changes in their lives, and in the lives of others. So, when they write about these fire-starters, there is something of identifying with their desire for God, and with the fact that ordinary people engage extraordinary life-change. And that inspires! So be prepared to be inspired as you read this book. Most of the names you will know, but what you will discover is how God set each, very ordinary person on fire.

—Steve Almond. Publisher, *Light Magazine*

Steeped in the Grace of God and rich history of previous revivals, *God's Firestarters* beckons all who long for the coming world revival, but more importantly in our individual lives and churches.

If you long for God's intervention, *God's Firestarters* is a book you won't want to put down. May God bless you as story after story of past revivals and heroes of the Faith will stir your heart for a mighty move of God in your life, in your church and for the coming world revival.

—Rev. Keith Bird, Chaplain & Editor, Order of St. Luke the Physician Canada

God's Firestarters contains valuable accounts of many of the most influential leaders of Christian renewal in the past five hundred years. From Katharina Luther to General William and Catherine Booth to J.I. Packer and so on, Rev. Dr. Ed and his wife Janice Hird have written excellent accounts of the life stories of Christians whom we should be very knowledgeable about in our present day and age. Indeed, as the Hirds challenge us, we should be emulating those tireless, courageous, visionary workers for the Lord Jesus as we navigate our way through the delicate and sensitive intricacies of our modern times.

—John Cline, Pastor, McLaurin Memorial Baptist Church, Edmonton, Alberta

Ed and Janice Hird have written a gem! They have captured elements of well-known Christian Leaders that reflect their humanity, consecration and influence. Ed and Janice have made these larger-than-life heroes of the Faith relatable. Rather than a dry historic hagiography, they made these figures come alive. One thing I was left with - in the Lord, I too may aspire to a life that glorifies God, blesses those around me and impacts in a significant way!

—The Rev'd. Dr. John Roddam, Anglican Priest, Release Ministries

THIS BOOK IS DEDICATED WITH THANKSGIVING
TO THE MEMORY OF ONE OF OUR 21ST CENTURY
GREATEST FIRESTARTERS, THE BELOVED

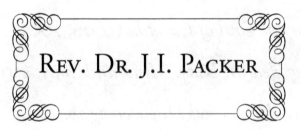

REV. DR. J.I. PACKER

He graciously wrote the foreword to two of
our earlier books. We miss him deeply. In
his humility, few of us realized how deeply
that he was impacting us, leaving us with
a longing for revival, Christlikeness, and
biblical transformation. As a true spiritual
father, he poured into us and wonderfully
disrupted our small and safe lives. To know
Jim was to be deeply stretched and forever
changed. May we be that generation that
Packer dreamed of, a firestarter generation
that truly knows God and makes him
known to the ends of the earth.

By the same authors
(Rev. Dr. Ed & Janice Hird)

from the Book Series
STRENGTHENING A NEW GENERATION OF HEALTHY LEADERS

Battle for the Soul of Canada (2006, 2007)

Restoring Health: Body, Mind and Spirit (2014)

For Better, For Worse: Discovering the

Keys to a Lasting Relationship (2018)

Blue Sky, a novel on family reconciliation (2019)

all available on Amazon or in many local Christian bookstores

God's Firestarters: Preparing our families for coming revivals

Published by His Publishing Group

ISBN 978-0-9782022-7-9

eBook ISBN 978-0-9782022-8-6

Copyright @ 2021 –Rev. Dr. Ed and Janice Hird

Library of Congress Control Number: 2021918728

First printing, 2021

HISPUBLISHING GROUP

4310 Wiley Post Rd. Suite 201
Addison, TX 75001
Ph 888.311.0811 Fax 214.856.8256

His Publishing Group is a division of Human Improvement Specialists, LLC.
For information, visit www.hispubg.com or contact publisher at info@hispubg.com

Book design by Wm. Glasgow Design, Abbotsford, BC.
Printed in the United States of America (and in Canada)

Table of Contents

Foreword

by Roberts Liardon

Each of us are alive at a specific time for a specific purpose — not born by accident or by mere physical choice. We are born when God decides that this is our time to live and do a specific work on the earth.

The range and variety of all our individual assignments is greater than our natural minds can comprehend. But this one common factor we can be assured of: God is always seeking for a man or woman to do His will and help change the heart of man.

That's what makes Ed and Janice Hird's book God's Firestarters so compelling. Within these pages, you'll find 20 unique journeys, spanning six centuries, of individuals who powerfully fit that description.

These men and women, along with their families, forged through a wide range of challenges and hardships together without giving up. Each in his or her own way helped bring the fire of God's truth to hungry hearts and to places barren of a move of His Spirit. Each had a part to play according to his or her own giftings and assignment. And as a result of their strength of conviction to follow Jesus Christ and obey what He had asked them to do, each in some way advanced God's Kingdom for generations to come.

Some of the men and women included in this book you will likely recognize; others may be unfamiliar to you. But in each chapter, the Hirds have succeeded in drawing out little-known details that bring color and depth to the journeys of these "firestarters." You'll see that, despite their many differences, they were all simply men and women who chose to do whatever God asked them to do, despite their own missteps at times and regardless the cost.

As you read, keep this question before the Lord in your heart: Why did You put me on the earth for such a time as this? You may already know part of that answer. Or perhaps you are only beginning to realize how critical it is that you seek the Lord for the answer. That's the key — to ask Him for the answer. When we begin with God, every work we attempt is completed with the accuracy of Heaven. It's a spiritual law you'll see played out again and again in the pages of this book.

We all have our place in the Body of Christ. Some are called to lead; others must hear from God that they are anointed to follow. Regardless, it requires more than desire to fulfill the will of God — it takes spiritual strength. And in the lives of the people represented in these twenty powerful stories, you'll find evidence of that strength in a variety of forms.

Don't read these stories lightly. Determine to allow the lessons learned by these godly men and women to become a "course" in your own school of the Spirit to help you stay on track. You have your own part to play; you have your own story to "write" for the annals of Heaven. So, through it all, just determine to keep on building your spiritual strength and walking out your own purpose in God. You're going to make it — despite any past missteps and regardless the cost!

Roberts Liardon,
author of *God's Generals*
book and video series

Introduction

20 Stories of courageous Christians guaranteed to ignite your faith!

I n *God's Firestarters*, you will discover little-known followers of Christ who confronted unspeakable evil, performed extraordinary deeds, started remarkable revivals, and changed the world.

Are you longing to experience spiritual revival? We all want to feel part of a greater purpose in life. But, how does God use everyday people to advance the Gospel?

God's Firestarters plunges you into the astonishing true stories of twenty heroes of the faith who lived from the 16th – 21st centuries. Journey with us as we explore the lives of Katarina Luther in the 16th century Germany, and Susannah Wesley in the 17th century. Rediscover the amazing impact of Susannah Wesley's sons John and Charles Wesley in the 18th century, and John and Mary Newton's love story in England. Plunge into the fascinating lives and marriages of groundbreaking 19th century missionaries: William Carey in India, Dr David Livingstone in Africa, and General William and Catherine Booth. Learn from the revival passion of Corrie Ten Boom, Aimee Semple McPherson, Chuck Smith, John Wimber and others in the 20th century, and finally J.I. Packer in the 21st century.

Do you need a dose of spiritual refreshment? Great for daily meditation and personal inspiration, God's Firestarters will stir your soul and awaken your heart. You will read about the remarkable men and women who give us hope that revival is still possible in our modern tumultuous times.

The best is yet to come. Thank you for joining us as we prayerfully prepare our hearts and minds for upcoming revivals.

Katharina Luther:
Reformation Fire Starter

(1499–1552)

"A wife of noble character who can find?
She is worth far more than rubies." (Proverbs 31:10, NIV)

Katharina and eleven other nuns escaped on Easter Eve of 1523, one of the few nights they were permitted to stay up late.[1] At the Cistercian convent of Marienthron in Nimbschen, Saxony, in the Holy Roman Empire (what is now modern-day Germany), Katharina von Bora was eager to be part of the new reform movement. Leonhard Köppe delivered herring in barrels to the Nimbschen convent, and secretly exchanged the herring for twelve nuns hidden in and among the barrels. It has been described as one of the most stunning jailbreaks in history.[2] A year later, a man was executed for aiding a similar escape.[3]

In 1524, the year after Katharina escaped the convent, Luther published a pamphlet: *A Story of How God Rescued an Honorable Nun*. This told the true story of a young woman named Florentina. She was shipped off to a convent at age six, and flogged and imprisoned in a convent prison cell as an adult when she tried to leave.[4] Luther also wrote about "children...pushed into the nunneries" by "unmerciful parents who treated their own so cruelly."[5] When these other nuns tried to leave, they would be arrested and even beaten. Luther commented, "...no vow is valid unless it has been made willingly and with love."[6]

Martin Luther's job was to find husbands for the escaped nuns, something he accomplished except with complicated Kate. She had become romantically attached to Jerome Baumgartner, a young man close to her in age. With many kisses, he promised her that he would return to Wittenberg and marry her. But his mother caught wind of this, and forced him to return to his home town. She did not want her son marrying a disgraced former nun with no dowry. At age twenty-four, Kate was considered to be too old to marry. Luther wrote Jerome on October 12th, 1524: "If you want to hold on to your Kate von Bora, you better hurry up before she is given to some other suitor who is on hand. Until now, she has not gotten over her love for you. And I would be very pleased if the two of you were united with one another (in marriage)." Jerome's parents instead married him off to a wealthy fourteen-year-old heiress.[7]

Luther then tried to marry Kate off to the aged Dr. Kaspar Glatz. She turned in desperation to Luther's colleague Nikolaus von Amsdorf, saying she would accept a marriage proposal from Amsdorf or Luther, but not from Glatz.[8]

Amsdorf met with Luther, saying, "What the devil are you doing, trying to coax and force the good Kate to marry that old cheapskate whom she neither desires nor considers with all her heart as husband?"

Luther responded, "What devil would want her then? If she does not like him, she may have to wait a good while for another one!"[9]

After Luther asked Katharina just what he was to do with her, she said, "You could marry me yourself."

This deeply shocked Luther, as he saw himself over the hill at age forty-two, as well as likely to be martyred. He consulted his father, Hans Luther, for advice. Surprisingly, his father wanted Martin to settle down and give him some grandchildren.[10] So Martin Luther decided to wed Katarina.

Five hundred years ago, Luther's Reformation allowed pastors (priests) to marry for the first time in over 500 years.[11] Marriage and family went from being second-best to something to be celebrated. Many priests' housekeepers with the priest's own illegitimate children were then promoted to become legal clergy wives. Some suggest that allowing priests to marry was even more shocking than the doctrine of justification by grace through faith.[12]

Many were scandalized that Luther not only endorsed pastors marrying, but took the plunge himself, marrying Kate in 1525. King Henry VIII of England, famous for marrying and divorcing several wives, ironically accused Luther of starting the Reformation out of sheer lust.[13] In 1527, Henry VIII sponsored a stage play mocking the marriage of Luther and Katherina — accusing them of spiritual incest in taking a monastic sister to bed.[14] A widely circulated pamphlet spoke about the married Kate Luther: "Woe to you, poor fallen woman" and "your damnable, shameful life".[15]

At age five, Katharina von Bora, because of her new stepmother, had been sent to a convent by her father. Her new stepmother didn't want any other children in the house.[16] The convent was run by Katharina's aunt. The nuns were pleased to receive future new nuns, and appreciated the financial donations from the young girls' relatives.

Years later, Martin commented about their getting married: "I never loved Kate then for I suspected her of being proud (as she is), but God willed me to take compassion on the poor abandoned girl."[17]

When Kate learned that she would marry Martin, she prayed,

> Now I shall no longer be Katharina, runaway nun; I shall be the wife of the great Doctor Luther, and everything I do or say will reflect upon him… It is like an assignment from God… God, keep me humble. Help me to be a good wife to your servant Doctor Luther. And perhaps, dear Father, you can also manage to give me a little love and happiness.[18]

After marrying on June 13, 1525, the Luthers made the former Augustinian Black Cloister monastery their home. Luther, as a former confirmed bachelor, commented, "There is a lot to get used to in the first year of marriage. One wakes up in the morning and finds a pair of pigtails on the pillow which were not there before."[19] Katherina also shocked Martin by putting up curtains and washing his bedsheets. He observed, "Before I was married, the bed was not made for a whole year and became foul with sweat."[20]

Katharina was a true biblical Martha, always working and serving her family. Drawing on her nunnery experience, she was up at four a.m. each morning, causing Luther to call her the Morning Star of Wittenberg.[21] She provided a financial and emotional stability in Martin's life that helped him be more grounded. Martin, being an ex-monk, refused to even charge his students for attending his lectures or be paid for his books.[22] He also was radically generous, even co-signing expensive loans on which others defaulted.[23]

Fortunately, Katharina was a gifted businesswoman, who turned their home into a profit-making hostel for students and others.[24] Luther commented, "I am rich. God has given me my nun and three children: what care I if I am in debt, Katie pays the bills."[25] With forty rooms alone on the ground floor of her Black Cloister home, Kate functioned as a Protestant abbess. She was busy with "a motley crowd of boys, students, girls, widows, old women, and youngsters."[26]

Kate and Martin had six children, two of whom did not make it to adulthood: Hans – June 1526; Elizabeth – 10 December 1527, who died within a few months; Magdalena – 1529, who died in Luther's arms in 1542; Martin – 1531; Paul – January 1533; and Margaret – 1534. The death of their daughter Magdalena at age thirteen was a great sorrow to her parents.

With her sheer energy, Kate gave Martin the local base for a global reformation.[27] In a 1535 letter, Martin wrote that his Lord Katie was busy planting crops, preparing pastures, and selling cattle.[28] She became gardener, fisher, fruit grower, cattle and horse breeder, cook, beekeeper, provisioner, nurse, and vintner.[29] Serving as Luther's publishing agent, she looked after the task of printing and distributing his prolific writings.[30]

Luther insightfully commented, "Marriage is a better school for character than any monastery, for it's here that your sharp corners are rubbed off."[31] Over time, they developed a very romantic marriage, as Luther commented, "Kiss and re-kiss your wife... A married life is a paradise, even when all else is wanting."[32] He began to write about Kate as 'my true love' and 'my sweetheart.'[33] In *Table Talk*, Luther commented, "I would not trade my Kate for France and Venice for three reasons:

1) Because God has given her to me and me to her.
2) I have seen time and again that other women have more faults than my Kate.
3) She is a faithful marriage partner; she is loyal and has integrity."[34]

"Kate", Martin said, "you have a god-fearing man who loves you. You are an empress; realize it and thank God for it."[35]

Sadly, Kate suffered greatly after Martin Luther died in 1546. Cast out of her monastery by militia and the black plague, she was forced to flee for her life. Her buildings, cattle, and beloved farm animals were all destroyed or killed. In 1552, while escaping from enemy soldiers, her ox-cart overturned. Landing in a watery ditch, she died shortly after.

We thank God for Kate's sacrificial leadership that helped bring worldwide change.

Richard and Margaret Baxter: Puritan Fire of Family Love

(1615–1691)

"Submit one to another out of reverence for
the Lord." (Ephesians 5:21 NIV)

Plague houses, quarantined by guards for forty days, were marked with a red cross on the door with the words "Lord Have Mercy Upon Us." Everywhere in London, the poor people were dying. In fact, they were forced back to the disease-infected city if they were caught fleeing to safety. In 1665, Richard and Margaret Baxter survived the Black Plague in the same summer that fifteen percent of other Londoners perished.[36]

King Charles II and the other rich people had all fled London. Only a small number of pastors and doctors remained to cope with the overwhelming epidemic. Richard Baxter commented, "The sense of approaching death so awakened both preachers and hearers, that multitudes of young men and others were converted to true repentance."[37]

Richard and Margaret, who had only been married three years earlier, were a powerful team caring for the sick and leading hundreds to Christ.[38] They saw the atmosphere change. Many mockers became converts. However, Margaret was severely criticized by her upper-class family and friends "that she busied her head so much about churches and works of charity and was not content to live privately and quietly."[39]

Richard defended her involvement in ministry, saying, "Does not Paul call some women his helps in the gospel?"[40]

Margaret's father, Francis Charlton, Esquire, was a wealthy leading justice of the peace. One of the traumas of her early childhood was the demolition of her home, Apley Castle, by Royalist troops in 1644, during the Civil War.[41] Men were killed right in front of five-year-old

Margaret.[42] Three other times as well, Margaret faced death, leaving her with PTSD symptoms for the rest of her life.[43]

As a confirmed bachelor, forty-seven-year-old Richard had surprised many by marrying Margaret who was twenty years younger than him.[44] Their unlikely marriage was a genuine puritan romance that we can still learn from over three centuries later. Richard wrote:

> When we were married, her sadness and melancholy vanished: counsel did something to it, and contentment something; and being taken up in our household affairs did somewhat. And we lived in inviolated love and mutual complacency sensible of the benefit of mutual help.[45]

Because of Baxter's dedication to renewing the Anglican Church, he, along with two thousand other Anglican clergy, were ejected in 1662 from their churches and forbidden to preach within ten miles of a local town.[46] He was often hated by the establishment and the jealous bureaucrats.[47]

As the 17th century's most visible pastor, Richard had been leading a spiritual revival in Kidderminster with his eight-hundred-strong congregation of weavers.[48] J.I. Packer commented:

> In 1681, when Richard wrote this 'Breviate' (meaning 'short account') of Margaret's life, he was probably the best known, and certainly the most prolific of England's Christian authors. Already in the 1650s, when despite chronic ill health, he masterminded a tremendous spiritual surge in his small-town parish of Kidderminster, he had become a best-selling author and had produced enough volumes of doctrine, devotion, and debate to earn himself the nickname 'scribbling Dick.'[49]

Baxter was a proponent of what he called 'mere Christianity,' a phrase that C.S. Lewis borrowed for his best-selling book.[50] He represented the often-ignored human side of Puritanism, how to be a Puritan without being puritanical.[51] Packer comments:

> The Puritanism of history was not the barbarous, sourpuss mentality of time-honoured caricature, still less the heretical

Manicheism (denial of the goodness and worth of created things and everyday pleasures) with which some scholars have identified it. It was rather a wholistic renewal movement within English-speaking Protestantism, which aimed to bring all life—personal, ecclesiastical, political, social, commercial; family life, business life, professional life—under the didactic authority and the purging and regenerating power of God in the gospel in the fullest extent possible.[52]

As a pastor and scholar, Baxter had the common touch, being able to connect at both heart and head level with both the humblest and the best educated.[53] Baxter held that "he is the best scholar who hath the readiest passage from the ear to the brain, but he is the best Christian who hath the readiest passage from the brain to the heart."[54]

Margaret, as an upper-class dilletante, was an unlikely convert.[55] Richard observed that she had in her youth been tempted to doubt the life to come and the truth of the Scripture.[56] She initially didn't think much of Baxter or the people of Kidderminster, merely attending church to humour her godly mother.[57] But God reached her and changed her life. As a new Christian, she almost died from tuberculosis, but the humble weavers prayed and fasted for her. God heard their prayers, giving her a miraculous recovery.[58] Richard commented:

And while we were all rejoicing in her change, she fell into a cough and seeming consumption [a wasting disease, such as tuberculosis] in which we almost despaired of her life… I and my praying neighbours were so sorry that such a changed person should be presently taken away before she had time to manifest her sincerity and do God any service in the world, that in grief they resolved to fast and pray for her. For former experience had lately much raised their belief in the success of prayer…But I was with them at prayer for this woman; and compassion made us all extraordinary fervent, and God heard us and speedily delivered her as it were by nothing or by an altogether undersigned means…the next morning her nose bled (which scarce ever did before or since) and the lungs seemed cleared, and her pulse suddenly amended, her cough abated, and her strength returned in a short time. [59]

Choosing to marry Richard was to choose a life of being persecuted. He commented:

> Another trial of her wealth and honor was when I and all such others were cast out of all possession and hope of all ecclesiastical maintenance; she was not ignorant of the scorn and the jealousies and wrath and persecutions that I was likely to be exposed to… To choose a participation of such a life that had no encouragement from any worldly wealth or honor, yea, that was exposed to such certain suffering which had no end in prospect on this side of death, did show that she was far from covetousness. [60]

As a wealthy heiress, Margaret loved to serve the poor and invest in her husband's ministry to the lost. She was full of love and forgiveness for all, including her sometimes awkward husband. [61] Richard, in mutual submission, wrote to Margaret:

> The Lord forgive my great unprofitableness and the sin that brought me under any disabilities to answer your earnest and honest desires of greater helps than I afford you, and help me yet to amend it toward you. [62]

In a neglected part of London, she founded a free school where poor children were taught about Jesus. [63] In one rented facility, over eight hundred were gathered to hear Richard preach. Suddenly the building began to collapse. Margaret ran outside, hiring a carpenter at that very moment to put an extra support in the building so that the listeners would not die. It worked. [64] Surprisingly, there were no deaths, so Richard was able to finish his sermon. The memory of this near disaster left Margaret with nightmares. [65] She was simultaneously very fearful and very courageous. [66]

Her husband, Richard, was frequently fined and then sent to jail for preaching the gospel. To keep the authorities from stealing her husband's many books, she gave them away to budding theologians, including those in New England, USA. [67] When Richard was thrown in prison, she cheerfully joined him there, even bringing her own bedding.[68] After building a church building for her husband, jealous neighbours had the visiting minister arrested, mistakenly thinking that they had captured her husband. Margaret generously paid the fine so that the poor preacher could return home to his large family. After being forced ten miles out of town in 1669 for preaching the gospel, the Baxters had to live in a dilapidated farm where "the coal smoke so filled the room that we were even suffocated with the stink. And she had ever a great constriction of the lungs that could not bear smoke or closeness."[69]

The Baxters entered marriage with their eyes wide open.[70] Packer has commented, "Vividly aware of each other's faults, they loved each other just the same, ever thankful for having each other and ever eager to give to each other."[71] Margaret was always trying to improve her husband for his own good.[72] Packer commented that she was reserved, intense, highly strung, restless, ardent, fearful, passionate and perfectionist, sad and self-condemning.[73]

At first, Richard saw his wife as too fussy about cleanliness. Why waste your time cleaning the house when you and your servants could read a good book?[74] But marriage for them was more about spiritually maturing than getting their own way. Richard commented:

> If God calls you to a married life, expect...trouble...and make particular preparation for each temptation, cross, and duty which you must expect. Think not that you are entering into a state of mere [pure and unmixed] delight, lest it prove but a fool's paradise to them.[75]

Richard wrote 168 books, many after his ejection from the Kidderminster pulpit.[76] Even though Baxter's books were largely forgotten after the Great Eviction of 1662, they were later rediscovered by John Wesley, William Wilberforce[77], and most recently by Dr. J.I. Packer.[78] Margaret, who freely spoke her mind, informed her husband that he should have written fewer books, and spent more time writing each book.[79] She also told him that because of his prolific writing and extensive ministry, he was not spending enough time in secret prayer with her.[80]

Margaret was a passionate prayer warrior who often out-prayed her academic husband.[81] Richard commented that his wife was very desirous

that we should all live in a constancy of devotion and a blameless innocency.[82] One of their marital joys was singing a psalm together each
morning and evening.[83] Packer comments that "…Richard was a public
man, a preacher and a tireless writer, constantly in the home but not
available to Margaret."[84]

Richard, who suffered from chronic pain in his later years, regretted
how it sometimes affected his temper and communicativeness around
Margaret.[85] Her high-strung nature often clashed with his intensity.[86]
Margaret was so afraid of getting cancer that she harmed her own health
in the process.[87] Packer wrote,

> [T]hey were both of fragile health, though in different ways,
> Margaret being a martyr to migraines and chest congestion
> and Richard being a veritable museum of diseases, which
> meant that he lived in some degree of pain most of the time.
> He was forthright and hasty, and could be strident; she was
> gentle and circumspect, and could not bear an angry voice.[88]

Richard was convinced from age twenty that he would not be long
for this life.[89] Baxter's physical ailments included "a tubercular cough;
frequent nosebleeds and bleeding from his finger-ends; migraine head-
aches; inflamed eyes; all kinds of digestive disorders; kidney stones and
gallstones." So, he preached and wrote "as a dying man to dying men."
Packer commented:

> Sure that his time was short and that there was a vast amount
> of work still waiting for him to do, he wrote at top speed
> and published with little or no revision, so that everything
> is brisk, frank, rough, and pungent, the literary legacy of a
> good man in a hurry.[90]

Because Margaret was very sensitive to loud noise, Richard worked hard
to modify his sometimes, hasty way of speaking.[91] Calmness was very
important for her sense of peace.[92] He greatly loved and admired Margaret, saying that she was "a woman of extraordinary acuteness of wit,
solidity, and judgment, incredible prudence and sincere devotedness to
God, and unusual strict obedience to him."[93] Richard was so secure in

his own skin that he honoured and respected his wife as a better pastoral counsellor than himself.[94] She in turn loved and respected him.

In their nineteenth year of marriage, Margaret took a turn for the worse and died. The bloodletting by doctors had only hastened her demise.[95] Richard was heartbroken.[96] As part of his grieving process, he wrote "under the power of melting grief" a book, *Breviate,* about his dear wife.

J.I. Packer believed that Baxter's book (renamed *Grief Sanctified*) can transform our marriages in the 21st century.[97] Packer described this book as:

> [A]n utterly fascinating pen-portrait, humble, factual, discerning, and affectionate throughout, of the complex, brilliant, highly strung, delicate, secretive, passionate, restless, loyal, managing woman that Margaret was.[98]

He saw it as a lifeline to the bereaved.[99] The pervasive denial of death in our current culture makes us vulnerable to great emotional dysfunction.[100] The Baxter's marriage represented a commitment to covenant relationship that brings a course-correction to our self-indulgent culture.[101] Marriage for Baxter was more about character development into Christ-likeness, than seeking one's own happiness and personal fulfilment.[102]

Packer commented:

> Richard and Margaret were what we would call 'difficult' people, individual to the point of stubbornness, temperamentally at opposite extremes, and with a twenty-year age gap between them; moreover, they were both frequently ill, and were living through a nightmarishly difficult time for persons of their convictions. For Richard, who was officially regarded as the leader and pacesetter of the nonconformists, legal harassment, spying, and personal sniping were constant, making it an invidious thing to be his wife. Yet cheerful patience, fostered by constant mutual encouragement drawn from the Word of God, sustained them throughout, and their relationship prospered and blossomed.[103]

Richard, in grieving the loss of Margaret, focused on the goodness of God in time of tragedy.[104] Rather than being resentful and bitter, he was grateful for the time that God graciously gave him with his wife.[105] Richard and Margaret's marriage demonstrate for the rest of us how to make it till death do us part.[106] God used the fire of the Baxters' love to transform many lives for eternity.[107]

May we too, in difficult times, trust that the fire of God's love will strengthen and revive our families and marriages.

Susanna Wesley:
Mother on Fire

(1669–1742)

"I ask you to receive her in the Lord... for she has been the benefactor of many people, including me." (Romans 16:2 NIV)

Pulling her apron over her head was Susanna Wesley's way of saying that she needed a break. She taught her nineteen children that she was not to be disturbed one hour a day for her personal devotions.[108] Born in 1669, Susanna Wesley was one of the greatest mothers who ever lived, raising up two of Christianity's most gifted leaders, John and Charles Wesley.[109]

Can you envision, like Susanna, being the twenty-fifth of twenty-five siblings?[110] Her father Samuel Annesley had a Doctor of Divinity from Oxford and in 1648 was chosen to preach at the British House of Commons. His eight-hundred-strong congregation of St Giles Cripplegate was one of the largest in London. Susanna's father did a remarkable thing at that time when he encouraged his daughter to read and study theology. When he died, he left Susannah his most valued possessions, which were his manuscripts and family papers.[111]

As a mother, Susanna prayed daily, "Dear God, guide me. Make my life count."[112] She loved to read biographies about other Christians, especially missionaries. While reading an account of Danish missionaries, she concluded:

> At last, it came to my mind, though I were not a man, nor a minister of the gospel...I might do somewhat more than I do...I might pray more for the people, and speak with more warmth to those with whom I have an opportunity of conversing. However, I resolved to begin with my children.[113]

Susanna believed that by first discipling her own children, she could change the world. As a young woman, she once said, "I hope the fire (of revival) I start will not only burn all of London, but all of the United Kingdom as well. I hope it will burn all over the world."

As the mother of the Methodist revival, she methodically instilled in her children a passion for discipleship and learning.[14] While only ten of her nineteen children survived to adulthood, she poured her life into them, raising up three sons, Samuel, John and Charles, to become pastors. Of her nine children who died as infants, four were sets of twins. When her maid rolled over while sleeping, she accidentally suffocated one baby. You can imagine the pain and grief that Susanna experienced from this.

Susanna believed each child was equally valuable and had an uncanny way of making each know they were important.[15] Some authors even see her as the mother of the homeschooling movement.[16] In an age when many parents only educated their sons, Susanna also taught all of her seven surviving daughters to read, write and reason.[17] She instructed all of her children for three hours in the morning and three hours in the afternoon. Her children began and ended each school day by singing a psalm and reading from the Bible.[18] Remarkably, she spent one hour a week with each of her children in personal instruction. Her educational goal was that on her last day, she would be able to say:

> Lord, here are the children which Thou hast given me, of which I have lost none by my ill example, not by neglecting to install in their minds, in their early years, the principles of Thy true religion and virtue.[19]

When Susanna failed to find adequate Christ-centered textbooks for children, she decided to write her own. Her first book, *A Manual of Natural Theory*, looked at how the natural universe revealed God as creator. Her second book was an exposition of the Apostles' Creed, looking at the essentials of the Christian faith. Her third book opened up the practical implications of the Ten Commandments for daily living.[20]

As both the daughter and the wife of a clergyman, Susanna understood the financial challenges of pastoral ministry. There was never enough money to feed and clothe the children properly. Her husband,

Reverend Samuel Wesley, as the underpaid Rector of Epworth and Wroot, was always in debt, and even ended up twice in debtors' prison.[121] Susanna offered to pawn her own wedding ring so that he could get out of prison, but her husband declined her sacrifice.

Because of Susanna's refusal to say amen to her husband's 1701 prayer for the new King William of Orange, he abandoned his wife. John, the fifteenth child, and Charles, the eighteenth child of nineteen were almost not conceived.[122] She was loyal to the Scottish Stuart Kings. As Susanna saw the new King William as a usurper, her husband left home, refusing to return: "We must part for if we have two kings, we must have two beds."[123]

To her friend Lady Yarborough, she wrote: "[H]e will not live with me... [Since] I'm willing to let him quietly enjoy his opinions, he ought not to deprive me of my little liberty of conscience."[124] Samuel only returned and reconciled after their house burnt down.

Being very outspoken, her husband had many enemies during his thirty-nine years in Epworth. Some of these opponents destroyed the Wesley's crops, stabbed their cows, attacked their dog, and set their house on fire in 1702.[125] Then during the contentious 1705 election, a political mob surrounded their house at night with loud drumming, firing of pistols, shouting that they would kill Samuel.[126] When their house was burnt down for a second time in 1709, six-year-old John was miraculously rescued from the fire. Susanna used to speak of her son John (Jacky) as her "brand plucked from the burning." Following the fire, she made a pledge: "I do intend to be more especially careful of the soul of this child."[127]

While her husband was away in 1711, she started Sunday evening devotions for her children, which unexpectedly attracted many neighbours: "Last Sunday I believe we had above two hundred. And yet many went away, for want of room to stand."[128] The replacement Epworth priest was deeply offended that far more people went to Susanna's devotional prayers than his Sunday morning service. This was not proper behaviour for a respectable Church of England clergyman's wife. Responding by letter to her concerned husband, she wrote:

As to its looking peculiar, I grant that it does. And so does almost anything that is serious, or that may in any way advance the glory of God, or the salvation of souls."[129]

Later, when her son John Wesley preached to tens of thousands, he fondly recalled the earlier revival that happened with his mother's Sunday evening devotions.

When John Wesley felt called to ordination, his father opposed him but his mother encouraged him to pursue holy orders.[130] Susanna coached John and Charles in the spiritual disciplines while at Oxford, encouraging them to read the *Imitation of Christ* by Thomas à Kempis and *Rule for Holy Living* by Jeremy Taylor. After reading these books, John told his mother, "I have resolved to dedicate all my life to God —all my thoughts and words and actions."[131]

They had their mother's full backing when John and Charles decided to go as missionaries to Savannah, Georgia. Susanna said, "If I had twenty sons, I would send them all." John returned to England after his few years in the colony of Georgia, and began preaching in the fields. Susanna approved, sometimes standing by his side before tens of thousands.[132] She also encouraged John to allow unordained men to preach.

After her debt-ridden husband died, leaving her homeless, she lived for her final three years with her son John Wesley in the famous Foundry Methodist Chapel in London.[133] On her deathbed, she said, "Children, as soon as I am released, sing a psalm of praise to God."[134]

May our families, like Susanna Wesley's family, spend our lives on fire giving glory to God and preparing for coming revivals.

John and Charles Wesley:
Hearts Strangely Warmed

(1703–1791) and (1707–1788)

"Were not our hearts burning within us while he talked with us
on the road and opened the Scriptures to us?" (Luke 24:32 NIV)

I n the eighteenth century, many debtors were stuck in prison with
no way out. General James Oglethorpe, a Christian philanthropist,
rescued 10,000 people from debtors' prison. This left him with a
new problem. What was he to do with these unemployed ex-debtors?
He decided to recruit the Anglican priests John and Charles Wesley to
serve these ex-debtors in the new colony of Savannah, Georgia.[35] The
Wesley brothers, however, were idealistic Oxford University academics
with little pastoral experience. This led to many disasters.

During their four-month-long 1735 trip to Savannah, Georgia, the
naive but well-meaning Wesley brothers took over the only public room
on the ship with all-day prayers, Bible readings, and liturgical services.
This provoked great resentment from the majority of the unspiritual
ex-debtors who did not want religion shoved down their throats.

Two women on board, one married to the only doctor (Mrs. Hawkins) and one a widow (Mrs. Welch), made a game out of pretending to
be interested in Christianity as a way of flirting with the Wesley brothers.
The sincere gullibility of the Wesleys left them vulnerable to false gossip
and accusation. During this time, a sudden storm broke the main mast,
causing the English passengers to cry out in desperation. But also on this
ship were German Moravian people, John Wesley was deeply impressed
with their calm singing and praying during this crisis.[36]

When they arrived in Georgia, they encountered one calamity after
another. These two gossiping women from their ship went out of their
way to tell lies about the Wesley brothers, falsely accusing Charles of

sexual immorality with Mrs. Welch. The rigidity of the Wesleys in matters of church practice did not go down well with these colonists. One time, Charles Wesley, following the Georgian law regarding Sunday as a day of rest, had the constable put Dr. Hawkins in jail for getting drunk and firing his gun outside the church building.

Mrs. Hawkins threatened to shoot Charles Wesley unless her husband was freed. As he was the only medical doctor in town, there was no physician to assist a woman whose baby tragically died during childbirth.[37] The colonists blamed Charles, even threatening his life. His congregation decreased to just three people. It later was revealed that Dr. Hawkins was given permission to leave the jail, but had refused to go and help the woman.

General Oglethorpe believed the gossip and slanderous accusations against Charles, including that he was encouraging people to leave Georgia. Charles' punishment was to have no furniture, dishes or food. John Wesley came to the Island of Frederica and cleared his brother's name with General Oglethorpe. While picking up medicine for his sick brother, John was also attacked by Mrs. Hawkins, who threatened him with a pistol and scissors, knocking him down and ripping his cassock with her teeth.

Another reason why Charles returned to England in August 1736 after only a few months was how upset he was over the poor treatment the slaves received from their owners. Charles observed some slaves being burnt with oil, their ears being nailed to the wall, while being beaten senseless. The slaveowners were only fined seven pounds if they killed their slave.

John Wesley continued as pastor of Christ Church, Savannah. But in 1737, he lost favour with his congregation over his strict inflexibility. He refused communion or burial to anyone who was not baptized by an Anglican clergyman.[38] John Wesley was in love with Sophia Hopkey, but refused to become engaged to her, because he wanted to focus on reaching the Chicasaw First Nations. Sophia's family was very unhappy with John Wesley for making her wait. After she married someone else, John Wesley refused Sophia communion out of jealousy. Her uncle sued John for one thousand pounds for character defamation, challenging him to a duel. He had to escape in the middle of the night.[39]

On his return voyage to England, John famously said, "I went to America to convert the natives. But who will convert me?" During another violent storm, he was struck by the calm faith of the Moravian Brethren on the ship. The Moravians had a strong emphasis on missions, singing, and prayer. Attending their London Moravian chapel, his heart was strangely warmed, coming to know Jesus personally.

Through the influence of his good friend George Whitefield, John reluctantly preached outside, because the established churches closed their doors to him. Outdoor preaching was seen as an unforgivable sin. While John preached outside near Bristol, revival broke out among the spiritually neglected miners. John Wesley could tell that they were converted as he saw the tears causing white lines to stream down their coal-blackened faces. Sometimes his opponents attacked him physically, calling for his crucifixion. Wesley didn't let anything stop him.

Sadly, John Wesley did not have a happy marriage. Charles blocked John from marrying his beloved Grace Murray in England who had nursed him back to health when he was sick. Because Grace was from a poor background, Charles didn't think that she was worthy to be John's wife. Behind John's back, Charles forced her to marry another Methodist preacher.

In 1751, John quickly married on the rebound: a rich widow called Mary who already had four children. Charles tried unsuccessfully to also block this marriage. He never had any children of his own. John Wesley's wife grew tired of his constant horseback preaching, refusing to continue to travel with him. His wife was sometimes violent, dragging John across the floor by his hair, and locking him in rooms.

Mary Wesley was also very jealous of other women, leaving John temporarily in 1758 and then permanently in 1771. Once John started the Methodist revival, many women admired him. They also wrote him letters for advice about speaking in public for Jesus Christ which he encouraged but did not call preaching. John was like a rock star in that time period.

He reported in his journal about his wife Mary, "Finally she left for good. I did not forsake her. I did not dismiss her. I will not recall her." Wesley's marriage was a tragic example of William Shakespeare's aphorism, "Marry in haste; repent at leisure."

In contrast, Charles Wesley checked with John about Sally Gwynne whom he desired to marry. Charles and Sally had corresponded for a year by letter before their wedding. Both Charles and Sally were wonderful singers. She was even invited to sing for King George III. John agreed to take their wedding in 1749. This happy, supportive marriage enabled Charles to write over 6,000 hymns during this time of revival. Sadly, only three of their nine children survived childhood.

Through the Wesleys' influence, tens of thousands came to know Jesus on a personal basis. Many were supernaturally healed through prayer. Through attending weekly class meetings, the new disciples learned to read their bible and live a godly life. Through helping people give up alcohol abuse, spousal violence and immorality, the Methodist revival birthed the new middle class in England and North America.

Some historians credit the Wesleys with preventing something similar to the French Revolution from happening in 18th-century England. Instead, the Methodist revival peacefully improved the lot of the English working class. At that time, adults and even children could be legally hanged for 160 different offenses—from picking a pocket to stealing a rabbit.

In London, seventy-five percent of all children died before age five. Among the poor, the death rate was even higher. In one orphanage, only one of 500 orphans survived more than a year. Alcohol abuse was rampant, even among children, with over 11 million gallons of gin consumed in 1750. Charles and John Wesley believed that changed hearts could lead to a changed society. By setting many free from alcoholism and teaching the children to read, Methodism gave parents hope for a better life for their families.[140]

We are all indebted to the Wesley brothers whose followers brought revival to North America and the world.

George Whitefield:
Awakening to the Fire of Christ
(1714–1770)

"After they prayed, the place where they were meeting was
shaken. And they were all filled with the Holy Spirit and
spoke the word of God boldly." (Acts 4:31, NIV)

Have you ever heard of a pastor being hoisted through a win-
dow into a crowded church building? Because of his rock-star
popularity in both England and the thirteen colonies, George
Whitefield couldn't make it through the main church door.[141] He was
involved in the first Great Awakening, bringing revival to both Great
Britain and America.[142] When asked why so many people listened to him,
he replied, "Haven't you noticed? People watch fires, and I am on fire."[143]
Charles Spurgeon called Whitefield "all life, fire, wing, force." Martin
Lloyd-Jones said that Whitefield is the most neglected person in church
history. He was the greatest man that you have *never* heard about.[144]

Upon being ordained at age twenty-one, his first sermon touched the
hearts and minds of the St Mary de Crypt congregation in Gloucester.
People at this service spontaneously began to moan and weep as they fell
under the conviction of sin.[145] Critics thought that Whitefield had driven
some men mad as there was no room for emotion in eighteenth-century church life. In contrast, his own Bishop Benson of Gloucester
insightfully wished that the madness might not be forgotten before
the next Sunday service.[146] The so-called madness was actually people
waking up to the life-changing love of Christ.

While in Oxford, he became close friends with John and Charles
Wesley who helped him in the spiritual disciplines. The Methodist club
at Oxford involved Whitefield in constant fasting, visiting prisons and
hospitals, and persecution by other Oxford students. This led him to

the edge of a physical breakdown.[147] The Methodist club reached but a handful of students (eight or nine at once). These well-meaning students were striving unsuccessfully through their own good works to find God. Their club died away with the departure of the Wesley brothers in 1735.[148]

After reading the book *The Life of God in the Soul of Man*, by Henry Scougal, Whitefield became convinced that good works would not earn him a place in heaven. "God showed me that I must be born again,"[149] he wrote. Whitefield described his new birth by saying, "The Day Star arose in my heart."[150] Experiencing the new birth gave him a fresh love of the beauty of spring, he said, "I would be so overpowered with a sense of God's Infinite Majesty that I would be compelled to throw myself on the ground and offer my soul as a blank in his hands, to write on it what he pleased."[151] This new birth experience became the heart of an unprecedented evangelical revival.

Whitefield accepted the Wesleys' invitation to join them as missionaries in Savannah, Georgia.[152] He waited, however, for months to sail to Georgia with his patron General Oglethorpe. During this delay in England, tens of thousands came to hear him preach about the new birth. Many couldn't make it into the overcrowded churches where Whitefield preached an average of nine times a week. "[T]hose who did come were so deeply affected that they were like persons...mourning for a first-born child."[153]

After passionately preaching outside to 10,000 miners in Kingswood near Bristol, he wrote: "The fire is kindled in the country; and, I know, all the devils in hell shall not be able to quench it."[154] Whitefield became the Billy Graham of the eighteenth century, preaching that all people needed to be born again.[155] He was very countercultural, doing the unthinkable thing of preaching in fields, without notes, to tens of thousands. In eighteenth-century England, sermons were only supposed to be given inside church buildings. George Whitefield introduced his reluctant friend John Wesley to the scandalous practice of outdoor preaching.

One time, Whitefield was riding by on his horse during a public execution where 12,000 had gathered. He got up on a small hill and began preaching. Before he knew it, most of the 12,000 people moved over to hear him. One observer said that the crowd was packed so close that Whitefield could have walked on their heads![156]

It was not an uncommon thing for Whitefield to weep while preaching.[157] Bishop J. C. Ryle said, "Whitefield's soul was all passion, his heart was all fire."[158] Martin Lloyd Jones described Whitefield's preaching as "zeal, fire, passion, flame."[159] He sought to reach the heart as well as the head, saying that many people "were unaffected by an unfelt, unknown Christ."[160]

Not everyone was happy about this revival. The chancellor of the Bristol diocese, accusing him of false doctrine, prohibited Whitefield from preaching in public or private meetings, threatening him with excommunication if he continued his unlicensed preaching in Bristol.[161] Jealous merchants threw dead cats, blood, and dung at Whitefield in a vain attempt to stop his preaching. He survived several assassination attempts.[162] Once he was stoned until nearly dead.[163]

In 1746, at Moorfields of London, he began preaching at six a.m. to 10,000 people attending a sporting event. A recruiting sergeant tried to shut down Whitefield by marching his soldiers through the crowd. Whitefield asked his people to fall back, making way for the soldiers and then closing up again. Suddenly the soldiers were encircled within a mass of worshipers. Whitefield stopped preaching, asking his people to sing with loud voices. Revival broke out. More than a thousand letters were given to him by persons who were touched by the Lord that day.[164]

In Exeter, rioters violently entered Whitefield's Methodist meeting-house. They swore at the minister and the men present, kicking and beating them. Then they stripped the women naked, dragged them through a sewer, and attempted to rape one of them in the upstairs gallery. Whitefield took the perpetrators to court, winning his case, and then forgiving them. This resulted in a significant drop in persecution.[165]

On December 30th, 1737, he boarded the ship *Whitaker* for Georgia, praying: "God give me a deep humility, a well-guided zeal, a burning love, and a single eye, and let men or the devils do their worst."[166] On his way to Savannah, Whitefield had such a strong voice that when the two other ships travelling with them drew close, he was simultaneously able to preach to all the people on the three ships.[167] At a time when travel was precarious, Whitefield had seven visits to America, fifteen to

Scotland, and two to Ireland.[168] He commented that it was always on the ships crossing the Atlantic that he met the devil head on.[169]

Whitefield was the best-known person to have travelled extensively in the thirteen American colonies.[170] By 1740, he had become the most famous man in both America and Britain, other than King George II.[171] Reminiscent of the Beatles, he was the first overseas 'British sensation.'[172] Many American historians see Whitefield as America's spiritual founding father. They view Whitefield's revival preaching as unintentionally galvanizing the separate thirteen colonies into the forming of the USA in 1776.[173] Steven Lawson commented that the United States was literally birthed out of the flames of the first Great Awakening.[174]

At age twenty-six, Whitefield married Elizabeth James, a thirty-six-year-old widow. Whitefield intentionally did not get married until his friend Howell Harris persuaded him to wed her. Elizabeth wanted to marry Howell Harris instead. Harris refused to marry her as he wanted to stay celibate in order to continue his evangelization in Wales. She did not want to marry Whitefield, but was talked into it by Harris over a few months. It took her ten years to get over missing Harris. Whitefield was not attracted to her, as she was not good-looking, but he married her in 1741 for her strong faith. He hoped that she would be an encouragement to his ministry.

Rather than a honeymoon, the newlyweds went off on a preaching tour. After four miscarriages, she gave birth to their only child, John, who sadly died at four months. Elizabeth was so devastated by their repeated loss of babies that, after their 1744-1748 stay in America, she would never again travel with her husband. Whitefield commented that "none in America could bear her." Elizabeth believed that she was nothing "but a load and burden" to her husband.[175] Whitefield would sometimes be away preaching for two years at a time. However, after her death in 1768, he said that he felt like he had lost his right hand.[176]

He was radically generous. Sir James Stephen, author of *Essays in Ecclesiastical Biography* (1893) commented that, "If ever philanthropy burned in the human heart with pure and intense flame, embracing the whole family of man in the spirit of universal charity, it was in the heart of George Whitefield."[177] After a fever had killed off many of the Savannah parents, Whitefield dedicated his life to caring for their orphans.[178] Wherever revival meetings took place, Whitefield received offerings, including from Benjamin Franklin, to help with the most famous orphanage and oldest surviving charity in North America, Bethesda in Savannah, Georgia. Tragically, Whitefield was persuaded to have slaves in order to financially aid his precious orphans. He would do anything to help his orphans. This is a sad reminder that even very spiritual people can choose the wrong course of action. His love for his orphans had blinded him to the injustice of slavery.

After Benjamin Franklin scientifically established that Whitefield was able to preach to 30,000 without an acoustic megaphone, he became his book publisher, close friend, and ally.[179] They would come and stay in each other's houses.[180] When Benjamin Franklin appeared before the British Parliament, Whitefield strongly supported him, attending every session.[181] Between 1740 and 1742, Franklin printed forty-three books and pamphlets dealing with Whitefield and the evangelical movement.[182] He even built Whitefield a building for preaching that eventually became the University of Pennsylvania.[183] Benjamin Franklin commented:

> It was wonderful to see the change soon made in the manners of our inhabitants. From being thoughtless or indifferent about religion, it seemed as if all the world was growing religious, so that one could not walk through the town in an evening without hearing psalms sung by different families in every street.[184]

The Bishop's Commissary (superintendent), Alexander Garden, in Charleston, was offended by Whitefield's article challenging slave owners over their mistreatment of slaves, and by Whitefield's preaching both in other parish areas and among other denominations. Garden declared that the slave owners were going to sue Whitefield for libel. During his sermon, Garden attacked Whitefield, and refused him communion.[185] Then he 'dragged' Whitefield into an ecclesiastical court, trying to defrock him.[186]

Jonathan Edwards of Northampton, a co-leader in the Great Awakening, wrote: "Whitefield was reproached in the most scurrilous and scandalous manner...I question whether history affords any instance paralleled with this, as so much pains taken in writing to blacken a man's character, and render him odious."[187] Professor Edward Wigglesworth of Harvard, reminiscent of modern-day cessationists, criticized White-field in 1754 for pretending to be an evangelist, saying that evangelists had gone out of existence when the Bible was completed.[188] After the Great Boston Fire of 1760, Whitefield generously raised money to help Harvard rebuild its devastated library.[189] Such philanthropy softened the hearts of Boston citizens to the Lord.

Everyone had an opinion about Whitefield. His chief opponent was the minister of First Church of Boston, Dr. Charles Chauncy, a former Anglican turned Congregationalist. He accused Whitefield of enthusi-asm, a very serious charge in an age of hyper-rationalism where any emotion evoked fears of revolution and fanaticism.[190] There was even a theatre production, *The Minor* by Samuel Foote, mocking him as Dr. Squintum, because of his crossed eyes caused by childhood measles.[191] Kidd has commented that, "Whitefield has the dubious distinction of becoming one of the first people in world history whose personal life became a topic of rampant conjecture in the mass media."[192]

In reaching out to the Chicasaw First Nation, he debunked the myth that European *equals* Christian, saying, "thousands of white people believe only in their heads, and are therefore no more Christians than those who have never heard of Jesus Christ at all."[193] Whitefield did not let criticism stop him, saying, "The more I am opposed, the more joy I feel."[194]

On a Sunday morning in Philadelphia, Whitefield preached to perhaps 15,000 people. Then he attended an Anglican Communion service where Commissary Cummings publicly denounced him and his followers. Whitefield followed this with preaching a farewell sermon to an outdoor assembly of 20,000.[195] The relentless pace was brutal to Whitefield's health. At another time in Boston, Whitefield became very ill, intensely vomiting between sermons. He was feverish, dehydrated, and perspiring freely.[196] Whitefield had wanted to preach in Canada, but was prevented by his health issues.[197]

During his four years away from England, the *Gentleman's Magazine* and other English newspapers erroneously listed George Whitefield as having died.[198] Upon his return to England, he changed so many lives that even the English upper classes began to give Whitefield a hearing. Lord Bolingbroke, after hearing Whitefield at Lady Huntington's place, wrote, "Mr. Whitefield is the most extraordinary man of our times. He has the most commanding eloquence I ever heard in any person."[199] One Anglican minister claimed that Whitefield had set England on fire with the devil's flames. Whitefield countered, "It is not a fire of the Devil's kindling, but a holy fire that has proceeded from the Holy and blessed Spirit. Oh, that such a fire may not only be kindled, but blow up into a flame all England, and all the world over!"[200]

In his thirty-four years of ordained ministry, Whitefield preached more than 18,000 sermons to at least ten million people.[201] As over eighty percent of the people in the thirteen American colonies had heard him preach, he was better known than George Washington.[202] Dr. Thomas S. Kidd holds that "perhaps he was the greatest evangelical preacher the world has ever known."[203] Because of his speaking gift, Whitefield's nickname was the 'Seraph,' a type of angel.[204] He was once described at the time by English Prime Minister Lloyd George as the greatest popular orator ever produced by England.[205] David Hume, a famous agnostic, commented that "Mr. Whitfield is the most ingenious preacher I ever heard. It is worth going twenty miles to hear him."[206] Reverend John Newton said that there was so much traffic on the streets of London at five-thirty a.m. gathering to go hear Whitefield at six a.m. that it resembled the evening rush-hour traffic.[207]

In 1770, Whitefield died in Newburyport, Massachusetts at just fifty-five. Dan Nelson holds that "his overwhelming pace led him to an early grave."[208] Despite his disagreements with Wesley over predestination, Whitefield still graciously chose him to preach at his own memorial service. At that service, Wesley said, "Not since the days of the apostles have we ever heard of a preacher with the power and the might as George Whitefield."[209] When asked if he would see John Wesley in heaven, Whitefield humbly said that he didn't think so, as he expected that Wesley would be so much closer to the heavenly throne that he would hardly get a sight of him.[210]

Whitefield has been used to set many people on fire with love for Christ. Memorably, he had prayed: "O that I could do more for Him! O that I was a flame of pure and holy fire, and had a thousand lives to spend in the dear Redeemer's Service."[21] Whitefield was passionate about awakening people to the new birth.

We also need to wake up to the fire of Christ. We too need to recapture the priority of the new birth.

John and Mary Newton:
The Transforming Power of Grace
(1725–1807) and (1729–1790)

"In the same way, I tell you, there is rejoicing in the presence of the
angels of God over one sinner who repents." (Luke 15:10, NIV)

When John Newton was seventeen, he visited the Catlett
family, falling deeply in love with fourteen-year-old Mary,
nicknamed Polly. In his autobiography, he notably said:

> Almost at the first sight of this girl (for she was then under
> fourteen), I felt an affection for her, which never abated or
> lost its influence a single moment in my heart. In degree, it
> equaled all that the writers of romance have imagined; in
> duration it was unalterable.[212]

Mary also knew from that very day that sooner or later they would
become husband and wife.[213]

Being an only child, he was deeply loved by his godly mother Elizabeth who taught him the Holy Scriptures. She longed for her son to
one day be a pastor.[214] His mother's best friend had also been named
Elizabeth. They both agreed that their young children (John Newton
and Mary Catlett) should marry each other one day.[215] But sadly, Newton's mother died of tuberculosis in 1732, leaving him motherless at age
six. His father, a stern, sea captain, was often away at sea. Later, after
his father remarried, John was sent away to an abusive boarding school
in Essex.[216] Because of his troubles in school at age eleven, he went to
sea with his father for six voyages.[217]

In 1743, he was forcibly press-ganged into the Navy, which was a
common practice at that time. His captain was not pleased that Newton
kept running off to visit Mary Catlett. When he did not get back in

time from his leave, they threatened to kill him for deserting. Instead, he was stripped to the waist, tied to the wooden grating, and flogged with ninety-six lashes.[218] No one was allowed to talk to him for a week and he was demoted from midshipman to a common seaman. John was strongly tempted to kill the captain and thought about committing suicide. It was his love for Mary that kept him from ending his life: "My love was the only restraint I had left."[219]

Alcohol addiction devastated his young life. As he was so bad-tempered and rebellious, his captain traded him to a slave trader captain. Because John made up songs mocking his new boss, he was then sold to a slaveowner, Amos Clowe, in Africa. He became a slave from 1745-1747 to Princess Peye, a Sherbro princess in what is now Sierra Leone. She treated him with contempt.[220] All the other slaves, except him, had a hut to sleep in. After coming close to starvation, he found a small lime tree and started growing his own fruit trees.

Near the end of his time with Princess Peye, he borrowed a book on geometry from another slave-owner's library and learned how to do the math problems. When the slave-owner saw his math problems in the sand, he made John come with him to his factory and write a math test. As John was successful, he was allowed to work with the slave-owner's brother in his factory. There he was treated well again, with clean clothes and healthy food. John's father had asked a sea captain to look for John Newton, and miraculously, this captain found him. After John was found in Africa, he was set free and sailed back to England.

Back at sea, John was so blasphemous that once even his hardened shipmates threatened to throw him overboard in order to calm a dangerous storm. He was so hated by his fellow sailors that when he fell overboard in a drunken rage, their only attempt to rescue him was to spear him with a whaling harpoon, dragging him back onboard. From that day, he walked with a limp.[221] John Newton, who wrote the world's best-known song, *Amazing Grace*, was a slave-trading wretch for many years.[222]

Secretly he began to read the Bible, although it never made sense to him. One night in March 1748, at the age of twenty-three, he was on board a cargo ship experiencing heavy seas and extremely rough weather. Worn out with pumping water and almost frozen, he called out for God's mercy at the height of the storm, and was amazed to be saved from almost certain death.

Everything in John's new life was about amazing grace. It saved a lost, blind, wretch like him. As he wrote in his journal, "The Lord sent from on high and delivered me from deep waters."

As his famous hymn put it, grace led him home. At age twenty-five, John married his childhood sweetheart Mary on February 1, 1750. As they were unable to have children, they adopted Mary's two nieces Betsy and Eliza. Because John as a sea captain was often away from home, he wrote many love letters to Mary. Three years after her death from breast cancer in 1790, he published *Letters to a Wife* as a memorial to their marriage and as an example for other people to follow.[223]

While he loved his wife passionately, John often commented that his love for God had to be greater:

> You will not be displeased with me for saying, that though you are dearer to me than the aggregate of all earthly comforts, I wish to limit my passion within those bounds which God has appointed. Our love to each other ought to lead us to love him supremely, who is the author and source of all the good we possess or hope for. It is to him we owe that happiness.[224]

John believed that many failed or miserable marriages came from expecting one's spouse to give to them complete happiness:

> It is to him we owe that happiness in a marriage state which so many seek in vain, some of whom set out with such hopes and prospects, that their disappointments can be deduced for no other cause, than having placed that high regard on a creature which is only due to the creator.[225]

In 1754, John Newton suffered a stroke and subsequently gave up seafaring. Instead, he became a tide surveyor, collecting taxes for the Port of Liverpool. John Wesley and George Whitefield helped disciple him.[226] Newton saw Whitefield as the greatest preacher that he had ever heard.[227] At age thirty-nine in 1764, after studying Greek and Hebrew, he eventually became an Anglican clergyman, serving in the backwater town of Olney, sixty miles north of London.[228] With William Cowper in 1779, he wrote the first Anglican hymnbook. Two hundred and eighty of the Olney hymns were written by John, who produced one new hymn each Sunday.[229] Before John Newton's new-fangled hymnbook, Anglicans had only chanted psalms in church services.

His bestselling book *An Authentic Narrative* opened the door in 1780 to his becoming the Rector (Senior Pastor) of St Mary's Woolnoth Church in London. Newton joined the Committee for the Abolition of the Slave Trade. Newton's influential pamphlet *Thoughts Upon the African Slave Trade*, sent to every Member of both Houses of Parliament in 1788, helped convince many powerful people to lobby for change:

> It will always be a subject of humiliating reflection to me that
> I was once an active instrument in a business at which my
> heart now shudders.[230]

In 1785, he persuaded the young William Wilberforce to stay in politics, and joined him in his fight to abolish the slave trade. Being an ex-slave trader, he was able to prove how brutal and degrading slavery really was. Rusty Wright has commented that:

> Newton testified before important parliamentary committees,
> describing chains, overcrowded quarters, separated families,
> sexual exploitation, floggings, and beatings.[231]

Some wealthy business people defended the slave trade as both harmless to the slaves and essential to economic stability. They even argued that the African slaves preferred being slaves. On December 21, 1807, at age eighty-two, after helping Great Britain pass the Slave Trade Act, he died, entering into Jesus' nearer presence.[232]

No longer could new slaves be transported from Africa. But the institution of slavery still remained until Wilberforce finally had slavery abolished in the British Empire in 1833. On July 31,1834, over 800,000 Caribbean slaves were liberated. Slavery in the United States continued for another thirty-one years until the end of the American Civil War in 1865. Unfortunately, slavery and human trafficking still goes on around the world today with over twenty-seven million victims per year.

John's song *Amazing Grace* has become the theme song of freedom, being sung at Martin Luther King Jr.'s Freedom Marches, at the tearing down of the Berlin Wall, and the freeing of Nelson Mandela from twenty-seven years of being in an apartheid prison. John Newton is a parable of what amazing grace is all about: moving from death to life, from slavery to freedom, from selfishness to everlasting love. May we be too inspired by John Newton to choose the way of life.

William Carey:
Firestarter for World Missions

(1761–1834)

"Go into all the world and preach the gospel
to all creation." (Mark 16:15, NIV)

As a young man, William Carey was caught embezzling a shilling by his employer. Fortunately, his employer did not press charges. For such petty larceny, Carey could have easily paid the price of imprisonment, forfeiture of goods and chattel, whipping, or transportation for seven years to the plantations of the West Indies or America.[233] Facing his own selfishness, Carey turned to Jesus.

William Carey, the father of modern missions, had a humble beginning as a village shoemaker in Paulersbury, England.[234] He was fascinated with reading books about science and history and travel journals of explorers like Captain Cook.[235] His village playmates nicknamed him Christopher Columbus.[236] Carey said that, as a young person, he was addicted to swearing, lying, and alcohol.[237] A fellow cobbler, John Warr, began to share Jesus with him.

Carey had a quick mind and a natural love of learning.[238] He would have normally become a farm labourer, but suffered from a skin disease which made it painful for him to go out in the full sun. You can imagine how unlikely it was that Carey would end up in India with its hot, burning sunlight. If Carey's face and hands were exposed to the sun for any lengthy period, he would suffer agony throughout the night.[239] So instead of farming, he became a cobbler. While making shoes, he was able to read and pray. He learned to read the Bible in Latin, Greek, Hebrew, Dutch, French and English.[240] Through prayerful Bible reading, Carey developed a conviction that he was to go to India. His unimaginative friends and colleagues tried to talk him out of this unlikely fantasy.

Many Christian leaders in Carey's time were cessationists, believing that the Great Commission to disciple the nations was only given to the first-century apostles and no one else.[241] Ryland, a key pastor in Northampton, England, said to Carey, "Sit down, young man! When God chooses to covert the heathen, he will do it without your aid or mine!"[242] Carey's father Edmund wondered if his son had lost his mind.

He said to his father, "I am not my own nor would I choose for myself. Let God employ me where he thinks fit."[243] Carey's five-month's-pregnant wife Dorothy refused to go to India. He decided to go without her and took his oldest son Felix with him. But then his missionary partner, Dr. John Thomas, because of East Indian Company politics, had to come back to England before sailing away to India. Since by this time Dorothy had given birth to her baby boy, she grudgingly agreed to travel to India but only on the condition that her younger sister Catherine accompany her to help with childcare for her three-week-old son Jabez.[244]

With unshakable resolve, Carey went to India in 1793. Through teaching at Fort Williams College in Calcutta, he invested in young civil servants from England, helping them to have a good start in India. He later ended up becoming a Professor of Bengali and Sanskrit in Calcutta, India. Carey believed that the future was as bright as the promises of God. He had an exceptional natural gift for languages.

Unlike a number of his family members and closest friends, Carey survived malaria and numerous other tropical diseases. Dorothy, who was very emotionally connected to her family back in England, experienced persistent culture shock, health challenges, and psychological trauma in India. Within nine months, the Careys had moved six times and were very poor. Dorothy's sister Kitty left them to marry a British man working for the East India Company, going to reside in another distant part of India. The final straw that affected Dorothy came with the death of their five-year-old son Peter. Because of strict caste regulations, no one would help with a coffin or burial, so William had to dig the grave himself and bury his son. Only the five remaining members of the Carey family were allowed at the funeral. Dorothy, or Dolly as she was called, had what we would nowadays call postpartum depression and grief over her two babies who had died. Back then, the wife was supposed to just keep going. Dorothy could not read and never wanted to move to India. She was a homebody, and none of her family had moved from her village for generations.

Even though she was emotionally traumatized, she yet again had another baby boy. One wonders to what degree she was affected by the challenging spiritual atmosphere of the country. Dorothy claimed her husband was unfaithful and would run out on the street, yelling and physically assault him. English women close to her would believe her until she would then say that these very friends were also having an affair with her husband. Dorothy's illiteracy made it difficult for her to grasp how amazing her husband's linguistic ability was for the Christian world. Carey and his wife didn't really have anything in common. Eventually Dorothy became so dangerous to herself and others that she was kept in a locked room in their home. William did not wish to subject his wife to the inhumane asylum. She never did regain her sanity, dying several years later.

As a workaholic, Carey was always working on another translation or workbook for the Christian gospel. His first wife and three surviving boys suffered from his not being there emotionally for them. Other missionaries became substitute parents for his neglected children.

Five months after the death of Dorothy, Carey married his second wife Charlotte. She was a Danish woman who was a great asset to him in his written work. They had a wonderful life together. The other missionaries tried to dissuade him from marrying her so quickly after Dorothy's death but he refused to listen to them. Charlotte was the same age as him and they had a very happy marriage until her death thirteen years later. He then married Grace, a widow who was much younger than him but was a great help to him with his physically ageing body until his death.[245]

Some bureaucrats from the East India Company did their best to expel Carey and his team from India. Anything that might affect financial profit was seen as a threat. William Wilberforce, however, having finally abolished the slave trade, presented 837 petitions to the British Parliament representing over half a million signatures, requesting that 'these good and great men' be allowed to stay in India.[246] Carey's enemies attacked him in Parliament for being a lowly shoemaker. Charles Marsh, MP, castigated these missionaries as "these apostates from the loom

and anvil, these renegades from the lowest handicraft employments."[247]
Wilberforce however won the day in the Charter Renewal Bill 1813.[248]

Carey's motto was "Expect great things from God; attempt great things for God." Entirely self-taught, Carey impacted the emerging generation of Indian leaders that birthed the burgeoning modern democracy of India. Serampore College was founded by Carey and his colleagues in 1818. He produced six grammars of Bengali, Sanskrit, Marathi, Panjabi, Telugu, and Kanarese, and with John Clark Marshman, one of Bhutia.[249] He also translated the whole Bible into Bengali, Oriya, Marathi, Hindi, Assamese, and Sanskrit, and parts of it into twenty-nine other languages or dialects.[250] Scholars say that Carey significantly contributed to the renaissance of Indian literature in the nineteenth century. Sir Rabindranath Tagore in 1921 informed S. Pearce Carey that his great-grandfather "was the pioneer of revived interest in the Venaculars" of India.[251]

While an ordained preacher and a church planter, Carey was fascinated with all aspects of daily living. In 1818 Carey founded two magazines and a newspaper, the Samachar Darpan, the first newspaper printed in any Asian language.[252] He was the father of Indian printing technology, building what was then their largest printing press. Carey was the first to make indigenous paper for the Indian publishing industry.[253] He brought the steam engine to India, and pioneered the idea of lending libraries in India.[254] Carey also introduced the concept of a Savings Bank to India, in order to fight the all-pervasive social evil of usury at interest rates of 36% to 72%.[255]

Carey introduced the study of astronomy as a science, teaching that the stars and planets are God's creation set by him in an observable order, rather than astrological deities fatalistically controlling one's life. He was the founder of the Agri-Horticultural Society in the 1820s, thirty years before the Royal Agricultural Society was established in England.[256] Carey was the first person in India to write about forest conservation.[257] In 1823, he was elected as a Fellow of the Linnean Society of London, one of the world's most distinguished botanical societies even today. As Carey's favorite flowers were lilies, he had the honour of having one (Careyanum) named after him.[258]

Having a strong social conscience, Carey was the first man to oppose the Sati widow-burning and female infanticide.[259] Many Indian women believed that by casting their female children into the divine Ganges River, it would help them give birth to males.[260] Sati was finally banned by the Government of India in 1829.[261] He also campaigned for humane treatment of lepers who were being burned or buried alive because of their bad karma. The Hindu viewpoint was that leprosy was a deserved punishment in the fifth cycle of reincarnation.[262]

Carey loved India and never returned home to England, dying in India in 1834 at the age of seventy-three. Near the end, he said: "You have been speaking about William Carey. When I am gone, say nothing about William Carey—speak only about William Carey's Saviour." Our prayer is that we too would have the same fiery passion for world missions that William Carey had.

Dr. Livingstone, I Presume: Setting Africa on Fire with the Father's Love

(1813–1873)

"The good Samaritan went to him and bandaged his wounds, pouring on oil and wine." (Luke 10:34, NIV)

Chief Sechele of the Bakuena tribe in Botswana, upon hearing David Livingstone for the first time in 1843, said, "You startle me—these words make all my bones to shake—I have no more strength in me, but my forefathers were living at the same time yours were, and how is it that they did not send them word about these terrible things sooner? They all passed into darkness without knowing whither they were going."[263]

David Livingstone had originally trained as a doctor in order to reach China with the gospel.[264] When that door closed because of the Opium Wars, God opened another door in 1845 to Africa, starting in Cape Town, South Africa.

Many African chiefs heard for the very first time of the Father's amazing love through Livingstone: "Surely the oft-told tale of the goodness and love of our Heavenly Father, in giving up His own Son to death for us sinners, will, by the power of His Holy Spirit, beget love in some of these hearts."[265]

Livingstone noted: "Baba a mighty hunter and interpreter sat listening to the Gospel in the church at Kuruman, and the gracious words of Christ, made to touch his heart, evidently by the Holy Spirit, melted him to tears; I have seen him and others sink down to the ground weeping."[266]

Eager that his tribal followers would, too, become followers of Jesus,

40

Chief Sechele had to be talked out of forcing them to believe in Christ: "Do you imagine that these people will ever believe by your merely talking to them?"[267] One chief, Sekelutu, was drawn to Livingstone, but afraid to read the Bible in case it might change his heart and make him content with just one wife.[268]

While teaching on marriage in East Africa to thirty thousand people, we asked many Africans what they thought about Dr David Livingstone.[269] It was encouraging to learn how fondly he is remembered in Africa. Some other westerners may have come to exploit, but Livingstone came to bless and set people free from their chains. Livingstone prayed, "God, send me anywhere, only go with me. Lay any burden on me, only sustain me, and sever any tie in my heart except the tie that binds mine to yours."[270]

Martin Dugard holds that Livingstone was a man whose legend was arguably greater than any living explorer.[271] Against the backdrop of the Crimean War setback, England was ripe for a hero, someone to cheer for. Dugard comments:

> Livingstone reminded Victorian Britain about her potential for greatness. The fifty-one-year-old Scot was their hero archetype, an explorer brave, pious, and humble; so quick with the gun that Waterloo hero, the Duke of Wellington nicknamed Livingstone 'the fighting pastor.'[272]

Livingstone had the mystique of a modern-day astronaut boldly going into unchartered territory. Travelling, said Livingstone, made one more self-reliant and confident.[273] He only wanted companions who would go where there were no roads.[274] His books were bestsellers and his lectures standing room only.[275] Crowds mobbed him in the streets and even in church.[276] One poll showed that only Queen Victoria was more popular than the beloved Livingstone.[277]

Livingstone knew that the Bible changes everything, calling it "the Magna Carta of all the rights and privileges of modern civilization."[278]

Livingstone literally filled in the map of Africa, exploring all of its main rivers, covering 29,000 miles, greater than the circumference of the earth.[279] One of his most famous discoveries was Victoria Falls, which he named after Queen Victoria, on the Zambezi River, saying: "It had never been seen before by European eyes, but scenes so lovely must have been gazed upon by angels in their flight."[280] During his extensive travels, he suffered over twenty-seven times from attacks of malaria, being reduced at one point to 'a mere skeleton.'[281]

His dear wife Mary tragically died from malaria in 1862 while traveling with her husband in Mozambique.[282] Livingstone wrote in his journal: "I loved her when I married her, and the longer I lived with her, I loved her the more. A good wife, and a good, brave, kind-hearted mother was she. God pity the poor children, who were all tenderly attached to her; and I am left alone in the world by one whom I felt to be a part of myself."[283]

Livingstone had been lost for five years in Africa and presumed dead by many.[284] An American journalist Morton Stanley, originally named John Rowlands, was sent by the New York Herald in 1871 to Africa to rescue Livingstone. Two hundred and thirty-six days later, after a seemingly hopeless search, Stanley found him, uttering the immortal words, "Dr Livingstone, I presume." His discovery was voted the greatest 19th century newspaper story.[285] Stanley called Livingstone "an embodiment of warm good fellowship, of everything that is noble and right, of sound common sense, of everything practical and right/minded."[286] Speaking to the fifty-seven men carrying supplies to Livingstone, Stanley said: "He is a good man and has a kind heart. He is different from me; he will not beat you as I have done."[287] After returning to England, Stanley was initially rejected by the London Geographical Society as an imposter, until a letter was suddenly received just as Stanley walked out of the meeting.

In the meantime (three months after Livingstone had been found), Florence Nightingale led a fundraising drive raising four thousand pounds to rescue Livingstone, with a team that included Livingstone's twenty-year-old son Oswell. "If it costs ten thousand pounds to send him a pair of boots, we should send it. England too often provides great men then leaves them to perish."[288] Queen Victoria went out of her way to thank Stanley for discovering Livingstone, saying that she had been very anxious about his safety.[289]

Livingstone called the slave trade the open sore of the world, believing that opening up trade routes would eliminate it. Dugard noted that "slavery became the cornerstone of Portugal's economy."[290] Hundreds of thousands of Africans were exported by Portugal from both the east and west coast. Dugard comments that "Livingstone's antislavery speeches, it seemed, were offending Prince Albert, Queen Victoria's husband. Albert's cousin Pedro also happened to be King of Portugal."[291] Livingstone's on-location report of four hundred slaves massacred by slave traders at Nyangwe was key in ending the slave trade. He mistakenly thought that discovering the source of the Nile would open up trade routes for Africans, ending their dependence on the slave trade.[292]

Livingstone wrote, "It was suggested that, if the slave-market were supplied with articles of European manufacture by legitimate commerce, the trade in slaves would become impossible...This could only be effected by establishing a highway from the coast into the centre of the country."[293]

Being passionate about the Kingdom, he prayed, "I place no value in anything that I may possess except in relation to the Kingdom of Christ. I shall promote the glory of Him to whom I owe all my hopes in time and eternity." Dugard comments of Livingstone, that "it was his habit each Sunday to read the Church of England service aloud...he prayed on his knees at night and read his Bible daily."[294]

Dr Livingstone was one of the world's greatest medical missionaries, explorers and abolitionists.[295]. Having received the Royal Geographic Society's highest golden medal, Livingstone lived in an era where no occupation was more admired than that of an African explorer.[296] Sir Roger Murchison, president of the Royal Geographical Society, at Livingstone's Westminster Abbey Funeral, called it the greatest triumph in Geographical research that has been affected in our times.

People are often amazed at how Livingstone, who could have chosen a comfortable life, instead sacrificed his life to care for the African people. In speaking to the Cambridge faculty and students, Livingstone memorably commented:

> People talk about the sacrifice that I have made in spending
> so much of my life in Africa. Can that be called a sacrifice
> which is simply paid back a debt as a small part of the debt
> we owe to God that we can never repay?[297]

Though his body was buried at Westminster Abbey in London, his heart was buried in Africa, because his heart was full of Jesus' love for the African people.[298] Florence Nightingale said that God had taken away the greatest man of his generation, for Dr. Livingstone stood alone.[299] Our prayer is that we too may have Jesus' fiery heart of love for Africa.

General William and Catherine Booth: The Fire and the Blood

(1829–1912) and (1829–1890)

"Religion that God our Father accepts as pure and faultless is this: to look after orphans and widows in their distress and to keep oneself from being polluted by the world." (James 1:27, NIV)

Cholera: everyone's fear, and it was happening again. William and Catherine Booth were there to help feed, clothe, and care for the sick in the stinky, rancid streets of East London.[300] It was 1866. The incoming tide from the Thames River dumped sewage into East London's water reservoir. Almost 6,000 people died. Two years earlier, in 1864, Catherine and William Booth had started the Christian Mission in this part of London. Charles Dickens commented, "I consider the offensive smells, even in that short whiff, have been of a most head and stomach-distending nature."[301] The smell from the Thames was so bad that people became violently ill. The Great Stink was not completely dealt with until 1875.[302] This is where the poorest of the poor lived.

Catherine developed scoliosis curvature of the spine at age fourteen, and incipient tuberculosis at age eighteen. As a result, she was often forced to spend weeks lying in bed. She commented, "I can scarcely remember a day of my life which has been free from pain."[303] Nothing, however, stopped her passion to make a difference in the lives of lost and hurting people. As a vegetarian, she abhorred cruelty to animals.[304] If she saw a driver mistreating a horse, she would rush out onto the street and compel the driver to treat the horse more humanely.[305]

She had a strong Methodist upbringing, reading the Bible through eight times before the age of twelve.[306] As a preteen, she became concerned with the effects of alcoholism on the community, serving as secretary for the Juvenile Temperance Society. Her father, though part of a total-abstinence league, used to periodically fall off the wagon. Her father's alcohol problems made her more convinced about the need for prohibition.

At the home of Edward Rabbits, in 1851, she met William Booth, who, like Catherine, had been expelled by the Wesleyans for reform sympathies.[307] Revival had become suspect to the now more traditionally minded Wesleyans. William Booth was reciting a temperance poem, "The Grog-seller's Dream," which appealed to Catherine.[308]

Catherine, despite her natural shyness, would go to the slum tenements in East London, knock on doors, and ask them, "Can I tell you about Jesus?" Some people say that she was a better preacher than her husband William. She even wrote a 10,000-word essay, asserting equality for women in ministry. Although William Booth had initially rejected the idea of woman preachers, he changed his mind, later writing that "the best men in my Army are the women."[309] One of Catherine's sons later commented, "She reminded me again and again of counsel pleading with judge and jury for the life of the prisoner. The fixed attention of the court, the mastery of facts, the absolute self-forgetfulness of the advocate, the ebb and flow of feeling, the hush during the vital passages—all were there."[310]

Catherine Booth successfully lobbied Queen Victoria to support the Criminal Law Amendment Act 1885, "An Act to make further provision for the Protection of Women and Girls, the suppression of brothels, and other purposes," which, among other things, changed the age of consent from thirteen to sixteen. Three hundred and forty thousand people signed her petition to end the sex trafficking of thirteen-year-old girls.[311] Catherine Booth started the Food-for-the-Million Shops where the poor could purchase hot soup and a three-course dinner for just sixpence. On special occasions such as Christmas Day, Catherine would cook over three hundred dinners to be distributed to the poor of East London.[312] She became known as the "Mother of The Salvation Army." Queen Victoria noted, "Her majesty learns with much satisfaction that you have with other members of your society been successful in your efforts to win many thousands to the ways of temperance, virtue and religion."[313]

William, originally a pawnbroker's assistant, was a practical doer. In

1865, he preached from a tent pitched on a used Quaker graveyard in East London.[314] His passion was for soup, soap and salvation.[315] His motto was to "go for souls and go for the worst." Many of the local churches didn't want William's poor young converts because they would soil their precious seats.

In 1867, the Booths only had ten full-time workers, but by 1874, the 'Hallelujah Army' had grown to one thousand volunteers and forty-two evangelists, all serving under the name "The Christian Mission."[316] In 1878, William changed the name to Salvation Army, with all the converts becoming soldiers or officers. "Onward Christians Soldiers" became their favorite marching song.[317] Between 1881 to 1885, 250,000 people were converted and joined the Army.[318] More Londoners, according to an 1882 survey, were worshipping with the Salvation Army than all the other churches combined. In 1882, six hundred and sixty-nine Salvationists, however, were brutally assaulted. One woman died.[319] The taverns especially did not like the competition, and resented the Salvation music and street preaching.

Mrs. Booth designed the Salvation Army flag and bonnets which served as helmets to protect them from rocks and rotten eggs.[320] The *red* on the flag symbolizes the blood shed by Christ, the *yellow* for the fire of the Holy Spirit and the *blue* for the purity of God the Father. The *star* contains the Salvation Army's motto, 'Blood and Fire.' This describes the blood of Jesus shed on the cross to save all people, and the fire of the Holy Spirit which purifies believers. The Salvation Army uses this flag in their marches of witness, the dedication of children and the swearing-in of soldiers. It is sometimes placed on the coffin at the funeral of a Salvationist. Catherine had the Salvation Army flag brought into her bedroom as she was dying, saying "the blood and fire, that has been my life. It has been a constant fight."[321]

Catherine and William also revolutionized the notorious match factories. Women were earning a pittance for sixteen-hour days. The deadly fumes from the yellow phosphorus rotted their jaws, turning their faces green and black with foul-smelling pus. Catherine pointed out that other European countries produced matches tipped with harmless red phosphorus. The factory owners Bryant and May said that the red phosphorus was too expensive to make the switch.

After Catherine's tragic death from breast cancer in 1890, her grief-stricken husband William opened a Salvation Army match factory, paying the workers twice the usual wage while using harmless red phosphorus. He organized tours by MPs and journalists to meet the yellow phosphorus victims, and to see the new alternative red phosphorus match factory. In 1901, Bryant and May buckled under the pressure and stopped using the toxic yellow phosphorus.[322]

Catherine Booth had deeply loved the poor. "With all their faults," she said, "they have larger hearts than the rich." William said at her funeral, "She was love. Her whole soul was full of tender deep compassion. Oh, how she loved." [323]Catherine believed that "if we are to better the future, we must disturb the present."[324]

May the blood and fire of William and Catherine Booth's lives inspire us as well to disturb our present with love.

A.B. Simpson:
Firestarter for the Nations

(1843–1919)

"But you will receive power when the Holy Spirit comes on you;
and you will be my witnesses in Jerusalem, and in all Judea
and Samaria, and to the ends of the earth." (Acts 1:8, NIV)

I n Western Canada, many people attend the Alliance Church (the
Christian and Missionary Alliance, or C&MA), founded by the
unsung Canadian visionary, A. B. Simpson. He once said that people
"must always dream dreams before they blaze new trails and see visions
before they are strong to do exploits." D.L. Moody said of Simpson, "No
man gets at my heart like that man." Simpson was a man of the heart,
even experiencing what he called the baptism of laughter.

Albert Benjamin Simpson was born on Prince Edward Island on
December 15th, 1843, of Scottish Covenanter heritage. The Simpson
family had emigrated from Moray Shire, Scotland to Bayview, Prince
Edward Island, Canada. After the collapse of his father's shipbuilding
business in the 1840's depression, his family moved to a farm in western
Ontario. Reverend John Geddie, on his way to the South Sea Islands as
Canada's first missionary, baptized baby Albert and in prayer committed
him to future missionary service.

Fresh out of seminary in 1865, Simpson had accepted the call to
pastor Knox Church in Hamilton, a congregation with the second
largest Presbyterian church building in Canada. Over the next eight
years, seven hundred and fifty new people joined the congregation. Dr.
William McMullen, another Presbyterian minister, said that Simpson
"stood out at that time as one of the most brilliant young ministers of
our church in Canada."[325]

Unexpectedly, Simpson was then called to lead a Presbyterian Church in Louisville, Kentucky in 1873. The recently ended American Civil War had left much bitterness and division between the various churches. As a neutral Canadian pastor, Simpson was used to bring racial reconciliation and forgiveness among the churches. At Simpson's encouragement, the pastors went to their knees and poured out their hearts for such a baptism of love as would sweep away their differences. From reconciliation among the clergy came two months of continuous nightly gatherings across the denominations. As the pastors joined their hands together in unity, over ten thousand local residents joined them in regular prayer meetings, lasting for a year.[326]

Simpson's success led him to being invited to lead Thirteenth Street Presbyterian Church, a prestigious New York congregation. His wife Margaret was not happy when they moved from Kentucky to New York City. Louisville, Kentucky had been a positive experience for Margaret and she was very concerned that the big city would have a negative impact on her children.

When one hundred Italian immigrants in New York City responded to Simpson's message, he asked his church board to admit them as new members. His board "kindly but firmly refused" for fear of being overwhelmed by immigrants and poor people. Out of that rejection came Simpson's vision of a fellowship of Christians where everyone was welcome, regardless of race, income, denomination, or social class.

Simpson decided to abandon his security and reputation in order to start a community where all were welcome in Christ. Leaving his secure pastoral position, he began afresh with just seven other people in a poorly heated dance hall. It was an unlikely new beginning. Simpson however had recently discovered an inner strength and resilience that kept him from slipping into discouragement. In the past, he had been such a workaholic that he had destroyed his health. His medical doctor had given him three months to live. But upon meeting an Episcopalian (Anglican) physician, Dr. Charles Cullis, at Old Orchard Camp in Maine, he experienced a remarkable healing of his heart. The next day, Simpson was able to climb a 3,000-foot mountain.

His new fascination with the healing ministry scared his wife Margaret when their daughter became ill. Fortunately, Simpson successfully prayed for his daughter Margaret's healing from diphtheria—the very disease which had earlier killed his son Melville. Sadly, his assistant's son died after his father only relied on prayer, trying to be like Simpson. After this shocking death, A. B. Simpson clarified that there was still a place for taking your children to medical doctors.

Word spread fast of these healings in 1881. He was besieged by many with pleas for help. By others, he was vilified and ridiculed as another quack miracle worker. Despite such criticism, Simpson received strong support from medical doctors like Dr. Jenny Trout, the first female doctor and surgeon in Canada, Dr. Robert Glover from Toronto, and Dr. Lilian Yeomans, a Canadian-born surgeon in Michigan. He also received much encouragement from well-known Canadian Anglican priests like Dr. Henry Wilson and Dr. W.S. Rainford. Many of Simpson's strongest supporters were Canadians, like William Fenton, Albert Thompson, and E.D. Whiteside, who had been divinely healed through prayer from cancer, tuberculosis, and epilepsy.

When Simpson started Friday afternoon healing and holiness meetings, they quickly became New York's largest attended spiritual weekday meetings, with five hundred to one thousand people in attendance. He even turned his own home into a Healing Home where people could come for prayer ministry. His loyal, long-suffering wife Margaret served in the Alliance movement as the financial secretary and for missionary appointment and equipment.

Simpson taught that "the great secrets of a happy and holy life are the Scriptures and Prayer." He was relentlessly Jesus-centered, as demonstrated in his famous 'Jesus Only: Himself' poem.[327] His passion for Jesus gave him a deep love for other followers of Jesus. Simpson had a deep love for the whole Christian community, regardless of denomination or nationality. He said, "I want to enjoy the broadest fellowship possible myself, and I want my people to receive the benefit of the ministry of all God's gifted servants, regardless of whether they agree with me in everything or not."

We thank God for fiery mavericks like Albert Benjamin Simpson, who helped tear down the walls of misunderstanding, bitterness, and mistrust between the churches.

John G. Lake and the Healing Rooms Revival

(1870–1935)

"Silver or gold I do not have, but what I do have I give you. In the name of Jesus Christ of Nazareth, walk." (Acts 3:4, NIV)

What if most of the people in your family died from incurable illnesses? Born in St Mary's, Ontario, Canada in 1870, John G. Lake and his family moved to Sault Ste. Marie, Michigan in 1886.[328] Eight of his siblings died, despite the best care from medical doctors. This family tragedy inspired Lake to seek the healing power of Jesus Christ. After he was healed in Chicago from a digestive disease, his whole family went from chronic sickness to supernatural health.[329] His invalid brother got up and walked after healing prayer, his hemorrhaging sister was healed, his mother was restored at the brink of death, and his wife was cured from tuberculosis.[330]

Upon being filled with the Holy Spirit in 1907, Lake said, "My nature became so sensitized that I could lay hands on any man or woman and tell what organ was diseased, and to what extent."[331] Reverend Audrey Mabley of Eternally Yours TV describes John G. Lake, a fellow Canadian, as the greatest man of faith for healing that perhaps has ever lived. For the first nine months after being touched by the Holy Spirit, Lake could not look at the trees without them framing themselves into a glory poem of praise: "Everything I said was a stream of poetry."[332]

Feeling a call in 1908 from God, John G. Lake and Thomas Hezmalhalch decided to take a ship to South Africa with their large families. Being sure that God would provide, they arrived with the clothes on their back and not enough money to enter the country. While they were waiting in line at Customs, a stranger gave them enough money to pay their way into the country. The family were then unexpectedly greeted in Johannesburg by Mrs. C. L. Goodenough, who offered a furnished cottage to American missionaries with exactly seven children.[333]

The only way that Lake could describe the anointing that fell on him while in South Africa was as "liquid fire" pumping through his veins.[334] Lake believed that the power of God was equal to every emergency.[335] The well-known South African author Andrew Murray commented of Lake: "The man reveals more of God than any other man in Africa."[336]

So many people were healed in South Africa that Lake was brought by Arthur Ingram, the Bishop of London and Chaplain to the Archbishop of Canterbury, to address a Church of England conference. Bishop Ingram said of Lake's Triune Salvation talk: "this is the greatest sermon I have ever heard, and I commend its careful study by every priest."[337] Out of this healing revival was birthed the Apostolic Faith Mission in Southern Africa, a movement now numbering 1.4 million people.[338]

Sadly, on December 22, 1908, while Lake was ministering in the Kalahari Desert, his wife Jenny died from malnutrition and exhaustion. She had been feeding countless poor sick people on her front lawn while waiting for Lake to return.[339] Her children were very upset by her death and some of her sons never recovered their faith after it.

Feeling a call to Spokane, Washington, Lake left South Africa, and then married a stenographer Florence Switzer of Milwaukee, Wisconsin, in September 1913. They had five more children.[340] Without her shorthand recording of his sermons, many of Lake's insights would have been lost forever. He commented of Florence: "Men in these days consider themselves to be happily married once. I have been especially blessed in that I have been happily married twice."

In 1914, he began the Spokane Divine Healing Institute, later called the Healing Rooms, training up 'healing technicians.' His instructions to them were to go to the home of a sick person and not come back until that person was healed. Some might be gone for an hour, some a day, and some for weeks.[341] Lake commented: "We pray until we are satisfied in our souls that the work is complete. This is where people blunder. They will pray for a day or two, and then they quit."[342]

Since he had previously been a manager for a life insurance company, his extensive business experience caused many business people to be more open to the gospel. Lake commented, "If there was one thing that I wish I could do for the people of Spokane, it would be to teach them to pray."[343] In Spokane alone, 100,000 healings were documented and recorded within just five years. One hundred and sixty-seven of the approximately two hundred people who visited the Spokane Healing Rooms each day were unchurched.[344]

Dr. Ruthlidge of Washington DC said that Reverend Lake, through the Healing Rooms, made Spokane the healthiest city in the nation.[345] This Spokane Blessing even spread back to Lake's Canadian homeland. A thirty-two-year-old Canadian, William Bernard, had been suffering from curvature of the spine since being dropped by his nurse at age three. When Bernard said that he had no faith, John G. Lake laughingly said, "I have enough faith for both of us." After his spine was healed, two physicians certified him as fit for military service. Bernard commented, "I've always longed to give my service to my country of Canada."[346]

Lake fearlessly submitted to a series of experiments at a well-known research clinic where they watched him through X-rays and microscopes in a laboratory context as he successfully prayed for the elimination of a leg inflammation in a dying man.[347] The Spokane Better Business Bureau investigated the healings, giving Lake and the Healing Rooms an opportunity to vindicate themselves by presenting numerous local healings with Spokane residents.[348]

Most of the cases where people were healed were ones that physicians had pronounced hopeless. One such case involved the healing of a thirty-five-year-old woman from a thirty-pound fibroid tumour in her abdomen. The tumour was completely gone after just three minutes of prayer.[349] Even the Mayor of Spokane publicly celebrated the Healing Rooms' measurable health impact on Spokane. Lake commented of the Healing Rooms: "The lightnings of Jesus heals men by its flash; sin dissolves, disease flees when the power of God approaches."[350]

Thanks to Healing Rooms International Director Cal Pierce's pioneering leadership in Spokane in 1999, there are now over 2961 Healing Rooms in sixty-nine countries around the world. Today, John G. Lake's life, through the Healing Rooms revival, still impacts millions of lives around the world.

Evan Roberts in the
Land of Revivals

(1878–1951)

"Repent then and turn to God so that your sins may be wiped out, that times of refreshing may come from the Lord." (Acts 3:19, NIV)

Evan Roberts had visitations from the Holy Spirit, showing all Wales being lifted up to Heaven. He was passionate about revival, commenting, "For ten or eleven years, I have prayed for revival. I could sit up all night reading about revival."[351] While preaching at Moriah Chapel in December 1903, Roberts said, "I have reached out my hand and touched the flame. I am burning and waiting for a sign."[352]

How might your own nation be different if ten percent of the citizens entered into the Kingdom of God in the next two years? That's what happened in Wales, the land of revivals and song. Born in 1878, Evan Roberts, the spiritual father of the 1904 Welsh Revival, worked from age twelve to twenty-three with his father Henry in the coal mines.[353]

For several months before the revival broke out, Evan would be taken up into the heavens every night where he would commune with God.[354] Evan began to ask God to give him 100,000 souls, something that occurred during this revival.[355] Revival historian J. Edwin Orr says that 150,000 people became members of local churches in Wales, with 250,000 becoming born again.

Prayer was the very breath of Evan's soul. He seemed to be constantly praying.[356] The prayer that Evan Roberts received from his mentor Reverend Seth Joshua was, "Bend me, bend me, bend us."[357] His theme was "Bend the Church and save the world."[358] He urged total abandonment to the will of God.[359] As one participant commented, "Did we not hear him time and again praying the words, 'Empty me! Fill me! Use me!' until they became part of our thinking?"[360] Whenever the Holy Spirit came upon Evan in a revival meeting, his face was transformed, bringing a radiant smile and shining eyes.[361]

The four "points" of Evan's revival message[362] were:

1) Confess all known sin, receiving forgiveness through Jesus Christ.
2) Remove anything in your life that you are in doubt or feel unsure about.
3) Be ready to obey the Holy Spirit instantly.[363]
4) Publicly confess the Lord Jesus Christ.

Evan Roberts became perhaps the most famous man in the world at the time.[364] The *Western Mail* newspaper said "His language...is extremely colloquial...There are no sprightly sentences, no sparkling epigrams, no melting intonations of the voice, but he speaks sense and to the point."[365] Participants said that it was not the eloquence of Evan Roberts that transformed people—it was his tears.[366]

Even the future British Prime Minister, Lloyd George, vouched for the authenticity of Evan Roberts and the Welsh revival.[367] Evan himself was only present at about two hundred and fifty-nine of the tens of thousands of Welsh revival meetings that took place.[368] The chapels were often so crowded that Evan had to climb over people's shoulders just to make it to the pulpit.[369] People were standing for hours in the cold, wintry air hoping that by someone leaving the church, they could push in to witness the scenes that were taking place inside.[370]

Troubled by both the adulation and criticism, he wouldn't announce his meetings in advance.[371] He wanted Jesus, not himself, to be the focus. Sometimes he would go to a revival meeting and then refuse to speak, instead praying silently before leaving. Evan said, "I am not the source for this revival. I am only one worker in that which is growing to be a host. I am not moving the hearts of men and changing their lives; but 'God is working through me'."[372]

From the very beginning of the revival, there was a strong sense of conviction of sin, with wrongdoing publicly confessed. Instead of football (soccer), the hot topic in the pubs was about Evan Roberts and the revival. The *Western Mail* newspaper stated that "the only theme of conversation among all classes and sects is Evan Roberts. Even the taprooms of the public houses are given over to discussion of the powers possessed by him."[373]

Drunkenness was cut in half, causing bankruptcy for many pubs.[374] Crime was cut in half. Former houses of prostitution turned into homes of heavenly singing, encouraging their former customers to go to the revival meetings.[375] The Bible Society in Wales could not keep up with the request for their Bibles.[376] People began to pay off their bad debts.[377] Some of the toughest characters in the Welsh valleys were converted. Pit-ponies could no longer understand the miners' commands as they had stopped cursing the ponies. The police, often having no one to arrest, would come to the revivals to sing in quartets.[378]

In one court case, the prisoner came under conviction, confessing his sins. The judge then preached the gospel to him, and the jury spontaneously broke out into Welsh revival singing.[379] Gomer M. Roberts commented:

> Who can but give account of the lasting blessings of the 1904-5 revival? Is it possible to calculate a sum total of family bliss, peace of conscience, brotherly love, and holy conversation? What if the debts that were paid, and the enemies reconciled to one another? What if the drunkards who became sober, and the prodigals who were restored?[380]

Just like with the 1970s Jesus movement, most of the Welsh revival leaders and participants were very young.[381] The revival services were marked with informality, laughing, crying, dancing, joy, and brokenness.[382] Many of these youth did spontaneous Jesus marches, singing songs and visiting the pubs to invite people to the revival. No one bothered about the clock.[383] People often stayed until two to three a.m. in the morning, and then marched through the streets singing hymns.[384] A participant, David Matthews, commented, "When I left the heavenly atmosphere of the church for home, I discovered that it was five in the morning! I had been in the house of God for ten hours—they passed like ten minutes!"[385]

As predicted by Evan,[386] the Welsh revival had a worldwide impact, birthing over thirty revivals around the world, including in China, Korea, India, East Africa, and the 1906 Azusa Street revival in Los Angeles, impacting hundreds of millions.[387] At one meeting, all Evan said was "let us pray," before revival broke out with singing, repenting, and many conversions to Christ. As with the later Korean revival, the Welsh all prayed simultaneously.

This revival of love gave Evan the ability to sing all day.[388] R. B. Jones, a Welsh revival leader, said of the singing, "The fact is, unless heard, it is unimaginable, and when heard, indescribable."[389] The first Welsh revival team was five teenage girls who would sing about God's love at the revival meetings.[390] The love song of the Welsh revival was the song, "Here is love vast as the ocean."[391] Evan told the reporters, "I preach nothing but Christ's love."[392]

Because Evan seldom ate, slept and rested, he soon succumbed to the pressure of his rigorous schedule. In 1906, he suffered a physical and emotional collapse, the first of his eight nervous breakdowns.[393] The doctor told Evan after his nervous breakdown that if he ever preached again, he would die.[394] He then moved to England, living in virtual seclusion until he died. Many felt that Evan was overly controlled by Jessie Penn Lewis, a critic of the Welsh Revival. Sadly, with her encouragement, Evan refused to see his family when they visited, only returning to Wales upon the death of his father in 1928.[395] While there for his father's funeral in Loughor, Evans spoke a few sentences and a "mini-revival" sparked. Evan Roberts died in 1951 at age seventy-two.

Imagine what God might do in your nation, if your people, like Evan Roberts did, bent their wills to God's will for your nation? Bend us, Lord! Bend the Church!

Dr. E. Stanley Jones:
Global Fire Starter

(1884–1973)

"They devoted themselves to the apostles' teaching and to fellowship, to the breaking of bread and to prayer." (Acts 2:42, NIV)

Who could have imagined that God would use Dr. E. Stanley Jones' book on Gandhi to inspire Martin Luther King Jr. to launch the non-violent civil rights movement? King told Jones, "It was your book on Gandhi that gave me my first inkling of nonviolent noncooperation."

While in England, Gandhi read the Bible for the first time, finding the New Testament compelling, especially the Sermon on the Mount. As Gandhi commented, it "went straight to my heart."[396] Because Gandhi daily read the Sermon on the Mount, Jones said to Gandhi, "You know the principles. Do you know the person yet?"[397] Gandhi confessed that he didn't but was searching.

In his lifetime, Dr. E. Stanley Jones was the most widely read spiritual author in the entire world, with twenty-eight books in print. Some sold millions of copies.[398] Jones was born in Clarksville, Maryland, in 1884. *Time Magazine* called him the world's greatest missionary.[399] In 1964, *Time* stated that Jones' "fame overseas as an evangelist is matched only by Billy Graham."[400] Many see him as the Billy Graham of India.[401] In his 1963 Los Angeles Crusade, Billy Graham spent ten minutes in the Crusade commending Jones's missionary work, calling him his "good friend and trusted advisor."[402] Mr. Graham wrote in his final book that Jones "made a profound impact on all those around him because of his extraordinary faith and service to others…His is a worthy testimony of living a meaningful life during the journey to eternal life."[403]

Early in his missionary service in India, Jones suffered a physical and emotional collapse.[404] Telling the Lord that he was done, he surrendered his ministry to Jesus, and the Lord miraculously restored him.[405] Self-surrender became his theme and song.

In 1930, Dr. E. Stanley Jones started the first Christian Ashram retreat in India, after spending time at Rabindranath Tagore's and Mahatma Gandhi's ashrams.[406] Jones said that only Jesus Christ was good enough to be the leader, the guru of a Christian Ashram.[407] He was very Christ-centered, teaching that the highest thing we can say about God the Father is that he is Christ-like. Inscriptions on the original Christian Ashram walls in Sat Tal, India, said, "Here everybody loves everybody," "East and West are alternate beats of the same heart," and "Leave behind all race and class distinctions, all ye that enter here."

Jones commented that in the Christian Ashram, barriers of class and cash disappeared completely. One man shared, "This has been the first week of my life in an unsegregated world. I have lost my resentment against white people."[408] There are many United Christian Ashram retreats across Canada, USA, and around the world.[409]

Jones was banned by the British government for six years during World War II because of his stand for racial equality and independence for India. His dear wife Mabel remained in India, looking after hundreds of boys in the Sitapur School.[410] Jones, referring to his many long absences from his family as an evangelist, commented, "Few women would have been equipped for such an adjustment and sacrifice...This was costly to my family—and to me."[411] When their daughter Eunice was very young, she asked her mother, "Which papa is my papa?" Their son-in-law Bishop Jim Matthews said that they had a Kingdom marriage, both living for higher means. Mabel said that she would rather have E. Stanley Jones for two weeks a year than any other man she met for fifty-two.[412]

In India, Jones had initiated "round table conferences" at which Christian and non-Christian sat down as equals to share how their spiritual experiences enabled them to live better.[413] Tom Albin said that "everyone was asked to share only their religious experience and specifically 'how religion was working, what it was doing for us, and how we could find deeper reality.'"[414]

While serving in India for over fifty years, Jones was personal friends with Mahatma Gandhi.[415] When Jones received the Gandhi Peace Prize, a top spokesman for the Indian government called him "the greatest interpreter of Indian affairs in our time."[416]

Experiencing reverse-culture shock while exiled in the USA, Jones spoke out against American racism on NBC radio:

> When I landed on the shores of my native land on September 7th, had I obeyed my impulses I should have taken the first boat back to India…I must confess I came to America with deep questionings and concern. From a distance your civilization seemed superficial and your Christianity inadequate.[417]

He told a critic, "If I should be kept back from India permanently, God forbid, then I should consider seriously giving the balance of my working days to help the (Afro-Americans) of America to an equal status in our democracy and to their fullest development as a people. For the color question has become a world question."[418] This time of exile also enabled him to transplant the Christian Ashram movement to Canada and the United States. For many years, Stanley Jones spent six months in North America conducting city-wide evangelistic missions and Christian Ashrams, and the other six months overseas.

Because of his global impact, Jones the peacemaker was invited to periodically meet with Presidents Roosevelt and Eisenhower, General Douglas MacArthur, John Foster Dulles, and Japanese Emperor Hirohito.[419] Jones saw everything through the eyes of the Kingdom, seeing inequality and racism as violation of Kingdom principles. He called the caste system "India's curse," similarly rejecting the curse of racism in his own American homeland. In a 1947 article titled "India's Caste System and Ours," Jones wrote, "The caste systems of India and America are fundamentally alike—they are both founded on blood."[420]

For Jones, the sin of racism had set back the cause of missions and democracy:

> There are no local or national problems any longer. Our treatment of the (Afro-American) is a part of a world racial problem and should be treated as such…You and I know that the central problem of Missions in the East is the white man's

domination. It haunts every gathering, public and private, we have in the East.[421]

He was one of the first in the States to have desegregated meetings, causing some people to gossip about Jones as a communist agitator. Jones also served on the Advisory Committee for the Congress of Racial Equality (CORE), which organized the Freedom Rides of the early 1960s.[422] *Reader's Digest* published an article entitled "Methodism's Pink Fringe" (February 1950), portraying Jones as a Communist sympathizer or worse. Jones responded ironically, "Breathes there a man with soul so dead, who never has been called a Red?"[423] Because of his connection with Gandhi, FBI Director J. Edgar Hoover had a 117-page file on Jones.[424] Since he led so many communists to Christ, the communist leaders were not very happy about him either.[425]

Jones was condemned for promoting social equality between the races. He replied, "If this be a crime, then so be it. It is a treason against democracy and against the Christian faith to advocate inequality of treatment between the races." When local laws required that blacks sit in the balcony, Jones instructed groups of whites on the main floor to move to the balcony themselves when the service began.[426] Jones was truly a global fire-starter for Jesus' Kingdom.

May we too echo E. Stanley Jones' prayer: "O Christ, set my heart afire with your love so that I can kindle others. Amen."

Aimee Semple McPherson, God's Dynamo
(1890–1944)

"Many women do noble things, but you surpass
them all." (Proverbs 31:29, NIV)

What if we told you that Aimee Semple McPherson was the
most famous North American woman in the 1920s?[427] How
is it that a Canadian farm girl, born in 1890, had such a
lasting impact on the lives of millions around the world? She was in
many ways the Billy Graham of the 1920s.

Pastor Barry Buzza, former National Leader of the Canadian Foursquare Churches commented, "Aimee Semple McPherson was likely the
most influential Evangelist/Pastor of the 1920s. She built Angeles Temple, the largest church in America at that time, debt free, and packed it
out four times every Sunday. I am inspired by the way God used a very
human, divorced Canadian woman, to fulfill a divine assignment."[428]

Growing up in Salford, Ontario, Aimee was raised in the Salvation
Army by her mother, Minnie Ona Pearse Kennedy.[429] Her father, James
Kennedy, was a struggling farmer who was fifty-six when she was born.
At age seventeen, Aimee said, "Lord, I'll never eat or sleep again until
you fill me with the Spirit of power."[430] Speaking in tongues for Aimee
was a source of strength but not of division. Having been touched
by the Spirit, she married a visiting Irish evangelist, Robert Semple.
They went together to China as missionaries. Aimee wrote, "I should
be willing to cross the continent upon my knees to say to one poor
sinner, 'Jesus loves you.'"[431] After both Semples contracted the terrible
disease of malaria, to Aimee's great sorrow, her wonderful husband
died. She came back to North America in 1912 as a single mother. She
wrote, "I had come home from China like a wounded little bird, and

my bleeding heart was constantly pierced with curious questions from well-meaning people."[432]

Remarrying on the rebound in 1912 to the practical Harold McPherson, she tried unsuccessfully to be the traditional stay-at-home housewife that her new husband wanted. It almost killed her. After ending up in hospital in Rhode Island, God told her to go back preaching.[433] Leaving in 1915 with her two children, she began preaching back in Canada. At her first meetings, only two men and a boy turned up for the first four days.[434] Aimee gathered a crowd by posing as a statue, and then inviting them to her revival meeting. After miraculous healings broke out, many curious people appeared. "My healings?" said Aimee. "I do nothing. If the eyes of the people are on me, nothing will happen. I pray and believe with others, who pray and believe, and the power of Christ works the miracle."[435]

When her husband went to Canada, seeking to bring his wife back home, he ended up helping her set up her tent meetings throughout the Eastern seaboard of North America. The sheer numbers of people healed during her services were astounding, including wheelchair-bound people being able to walk, and blind people being able to see.[436] After several years of itinerant travel, her husband Harold left her in search of a more stable life back in his home town. He divorced her.

The next step was travel to the West Coast in 1918. Aimee and her mother Minnie Kennedy became the first women to drive alone across North America on uncharted roads in the USA. On their way there, they saw many miracles as city after city opened up following the 1918 flu epidemic lockdown. After relocating to Los Angeles, Aimee became as well-known as Charlie Chaplain, Harry Houdini, and even President Teddy Roosevelt. Charlie Chaplin, who secretly visited the mega-church Angelus Temple, gave Aimee advice on a better stage arrangement for her illustrated sermons and dramas.[437] "Half of your success is due to your magnetic appeal, half due to the props and the lights," Chaplin told McPherson. "Whether you like it or not, you're an actress."[438]

In her autobiographical sermon "From Milk-Pail to Pulpit," Aimee dressed as a milkmaid with a pail of milk, asking the congregation, "Have you ever been to a farm?" Once she turned up as a USC football player to dramatize a sermon about "carrying the ball for Christ"; on another Sunday night she put on a policeman's uniform and stood by a highway patrolman's motorcycle to "put sin under arrest."[439] The BBC reported that "she had the best actors, the best set designers, the best costumes, the best make-up artists and professional lighting."[440]

It is hard to imagine that 25,000 people, nearly five percent of the population of Los Angeles at that time, attended her congregation. One month after opening Angeles Temple in Los Angeles in 1923, Aimee started L.I.F.E Bible College which soon attracted one thousand students.[441]

The *LA Times* wrote about Aimee as having "a spectacular career punctuated by romance, legal battles, adventure and tragedy."[442] After starting the first Christian radio station, she angered the LA crime mob and political bosses by having ex-drug dealers and sex workers give testimonies on the radio.[443] Not even the mob could intimidate her. Standing for her convictions, she spoke the truth and refused to bow. By her courage, she changed the world.[444]

After ignoring kidnapping and death threats, Aimee was kidnapped at the beach by the mob on May 18, 1926, and taken across the border to Mexico, a common hideout for LA kidnappers.[445] Presumed drowned, Aimee missed her own massive memorial service.[446] Upon hearing about Aimee's escape on June 23, 1926, there were spontaneous street parades with dancing and singing.[447] At least 50,000 people welcomed her back from her kidnapping at the LA train station.[448]

Sadly, Aimee had to then endure an exhausting ninety-day court case.[449] The paparazzi falsely accused her of covering up an abortion. Her medical records vindicated her showing that she had had a hysterectomy many years previously.[450] After her victory, Aimee commented, "You can imagine my agony at seeing my name blazoned forth in the daily press in so sordid a manner."[451] The relentless media mud-slinging was very harmful to her most intimate family relationships, especially with her mother.[452] Jack Hayford, fourth president of the Foursquare Church, said that "there are very few people who have suffered more unfairness and criticism for magnifying the name of Jesus."[453]

David Hutton, who became her third husband, scammed her and took advantage of her exhaustion, convincing her to elope to Reno in

1931. This marriage quickly collapsed after the discovery of his deceitful relationships with other women.

After her premature death by mistake from sleeping pills at age fifty-four, she left an enduring legacy as founder of the Foursquare churches. It now has over 75,000 churches, 8.7 million members and adherents in 144 countries. Aimee was an unforgettable worldwide fire-starter.

Corrie Ten Boom:
Impact Through Surrender

(1892–1983)

"Lord, how often shall my brother sin against me and I forgive him? Jesus said 'seventy times seven'." (Matthew 18:21-22, NIV)

In Munich, a former Ravensbruck guard who had tortured her said to Corrie Ten Boom: "How grateful I am for your message, Fraulein. To think, as you said, that he washes my sins away!" Corrie later wrote, "His hand was thrust out to shake mine… Even as angry, vengeful thoughts boiled through me, I saw the sin of them. Jesus Christ had died for this man. Was I going to ask for more? Lord Jesus, I prayed, forgive me and help me to forgive him… Again, I silently prayed 'Jesus, I cannot forgive him. Give me your forgiveness.' As I took his hand, my heart felt an overwhelming love for this stranger."[454]

After the Nazis conquered Holland, 100,000 Dutch Jews were sent to concentration camps. Corrie's father Casper, known as the Grand Old Man of Haarlem, had a deep love of Jewish people, saying, "In this house, God's people are always welcome." No one was turned away. Corrie similarly prayed, "Lord Jesus, I offer myself for your people. In any way. Any place. Any time."[455] Through the young men disguising themselves as Nazi soldiers, her underground team saved one hundred Jewish babies who were about to be killed in an orphanage.

A well-known architect built them a secret two-and-a-half-foot-wide hiding place behind a new brick wall in Corrie's bedroom.[456] Even after arresting the Ten Booms, the Gestapo were never able to find the Jews hidden in this 'angel crib' hiding place.[457] At the time of the arrest, Corrie's interrogator painfully slapped her in the face after every question. Corrie cried out: "Lord Jesus, protect me!"

He hissed at her, "If you mention that name again once more, I will kill you." But miraculously, he stopped beating her.[458]

Corrie, Betsie and their father all glanced at their fireplace's plaque: 'Jesus is Victor.' Corrie thought: "It looks now as if the Gestapo were the conquerors. But they are not."[459]

She and her sister Betsie hid over eight hundred Jewish people in their Haarlem watchmaker home before being sent to Ravensbruck Concentration Camp in East Germany where 96,000 women died. "The sufferings of Jesus," said Corrie, "became very real to me at Ravensbruck."[460] She lost four family members in the concentration camps, including her beloved older sister Betsie who forgave and prayed for the guards even as they mercilessly beat her. "Don't hate," Betsie pleaded to Corrie. Three days before Betsie died, she shared with her sister Corrie the vision of first opening healing homes in Holland and Germany, before going around the world sharing about Jesus' love and forgiveness. Two weeks later, Corrie was set free through a God-ordained clerical error.[461] One week after this, all the other women her age at Ravensbruck were taken to the gas chamber.

Upon returning to Holland, Corrie opened a home in Holland to bring healing for people, even including the ostracized Dutch who had collaborated with the Nazis. She was knighted by the Queen of the Netherlands for her work.

Corrie told God that she was willing to go where he wanted her to go, but hoped that he'd never send her back to Germany. Finally, after sensing a blockage in her prayer life, she repented, saying, "Yes, Lord, I'll go to Germany too."[462] God sent her back to Ravensbruck to lead Bible studies with former guards, now in prison. All she could see was aversion and bitterness. They saw her as theologically simplistic and uncultured. The Lord said the word 'chocolate.' Once she gave them chocolate, they opened their hearts to her.[463] Then she rented and cleaned up a former concentration camp in Germany to bring temporary housing and healing to some of the nine million Germans who had been bombed or driven out of their homes.[464]

Corrie became a penniless person as she mentions in her book, Tramp for the Lord, travelling for three decades to sixty-two countries, and sleeping in over one thousand different beds.[465] Wherever she went globally, Corrie shared from her Ravensbruck experience that the light and love of Jesus Christ is deeper than the deepest darkness. She was the favourite travelling companion of the Bible-smuggler Brother Andrew as they both did missionary work behind the Iron Curtain in Vietnam and twelve other Communist countries. In Vietnam, they gave her the honorific title of "Double-old Grandmother."[466] While in the Soviet Union, she intentionally preached the gospel in her hotel room, knowing that everything she said was being listened to and recorded by communist officials.

Corrie was a unique blend of the compassion of a Mother Theresa and the evangelistic passion of Billy Graham. Through her deep friendship with Reverend Billy and Ruth Graham, Corrie's book *The Hiding Place* was turned into a movie which reached tens of millions. Ruth Graham said, "I didn't know anyone who had suffered so intensely for the Lord and for his people, as Corrie had, and come through with absolutely nothing but love in her heart for her captors—she forgave them."[467]

In 1967, Corrie was recognized by Israel as a righteous gentile. A tree was planted in her honour.[468] When people kept telling her how brave she was, Corrie transparently prayed,

> What little courage I have…I was not brave. I was often like a timid, fluttering bird, looking for a hiding place…Lord, I am weak and cowardly and of little faith; do hold me close. Thou art the conqueror. May that assurance give me courage and loyalty.[469]

Speaking in an African prison, Corrie said about Ravensbruck, "I knew that unforgiveness would do more harm than the guard's whip…I could not do it. I was not able. Jesus in me was able to do it. You see, you never touch the ocean of God's love as when you love your enemies."[470] When Corrie shared with prisoners in Rwanda, a revival of joy and hope broke out, even among the guards. As she was leaving, the prisoners swarmed around her, chanting "Old woman, come back. Old woman, come back and tell us more of Jesus."[471] Many people are unaware of the powerful international healing ministry that Corrie had, once even healing a leper in Vellore, India, through laying on of her hands.[472]

Because of her work blessing indigenous people, Corrie was adopted into the Hopi First Nation and given the name Beautiful Flower.[473] While staying at a Kansas farm, Corrie challenged her host. He had recently kicked his son out, telling him to never darken his doorstep again. She said to the farmer,

> If you believe in Jesus Christ and belong to Him, your sins have been cast into the depths of the sea, and that's very deep. But then he expects also that you forgive the sins of your boy and cast them into the depths of the sea. Just imagine how you would feel if there should be another war, if your son had to go back into service and was killed in action. Don't you think you should forgive him right now?

After riding together in silence, the farmer invited Corrie to go with him where he asked his son to forgive him. His son replied, "But, Father. I should ask you for forgiveness."[474]

In her late sixties, Corrie was betrayed and hurt by some Christians she loved and trusted. "You would have thought that, having been able to forgive the guards in Ravensbruck, forgiving Christian friends would be child's play. It wasn't. For weeks, I seethed inside. But at last, I asked God again to work His miracle in me...I was restored to the Father." She later burnt the painful letters from her friends, as a sign of letting go.[475]

Are you willing, like Corrie, to find victory through surrendering your unforgiveness?

C.S. Lewis:
Surprised by the Fire
(1898–1963)

"Love the Lord your God with all your heart and all your soul and all your mind." (Matthew 22:37, NIV)

On Sunday, December 6, 1914, C.S. Lewis, a confirmed atheist, was confirmed in the Church of Ireland at age sixteen in order to avoid a fight with his father, "one of the worse acts of his life."[476] Confirmation in the Church was outwardly an affirmation of one's Christian faith. He later commented, "Cowardice drove me into hypocrisy and hypocrisy into blasphemy."[477]

At age seventeen, C.S. Lewis explained bluntly to a Christian friend he'd known since childhood, "I believe in no religion. There is absolutely no proof for any of them, and from a philosophical standpoint, Christianity is not even the best."[478] One of his prep school friends described C.S. "Jack" as a "riotously amusing atheist."[479] As a teenager, he resented God for not existing, and for creating such a flawed world.[480] Just after World War I, Lewis, a wounded veteran, boasted that during his time in the trenches, he "never sank so low as to pray." To a friend about the same time, he said, "You take too many things for granted. You can't start with God. I don't accept God!"[481]

His father Albert, like so many even today, treated education as more important than family, with disastrous results. C.S. Lewis and his father Albert were like ships passing in the night, not knowing how to connect. Being very close to his calm, cheerful mother, her sudden death from cancer left ten-year old Lewis feeling like the mythical Atlantis was sinking.[482] He commented, "With my mother's death, all settled happiness, all that was tranquil and reliable, disappeared from my life…the great continent had sunk like Atlantis."[483]

Jack's mother Flora Hamilton, who tutored him in Latin and French, was brilliant, earning an honors degree in mathematics at Queens University in Belfast.[484] Her father, grandfather and great-grandfather had all been Anglican (Church of Ireland) clergy, the latter being a bishop.[485] As a child, Jack shared his mother's strong faith. It was like God had died with his mother.

Jack's secure Irish childhood dissolved into a nightmare of six years of painful residential school living in England.[486] He later commented that English accents at the boarding school sounded to his childhood ears like some strange demonic chatter.[487] Both Jack and his older brother Warren were traumatized by a brutal schoolmaster at their first boarding school Wynard in Watford.[488] Looking back, Jack would call Wynard "Belsen" after the Nazi concentration camp.[489]

In a letter to a young person, Lewis wrote, "I was in three schools (all boarding schools) of which two were very horrid. I never hated anything so much, not even the front-line trenches in World War I. Indeed, the story is far too horrid to tell anyone of your age."[490] Jack's second residential school Malvern was rife with bullying and sexual abuse.[491] After Jack threatened to shoot himself, his father relocated him to Great Bookham, Surrey, to be taught by a private tutor, William Kirkpatrick, who had trained for the ordained ministry in Ireland.[492] Kirkpatrick, as an ardent atheist, was portrayed in Lewis' novel *That Hideous Strength* as MacPhee, a humourless, free-thinking Ulsterman.[493] A few months before Jack's death in 1963, he stated, that after fifty years of struggling, he had finally forgiven the headmaster Capron who had so damaged his earliest boyhood.[494]

His father Albert was so swallowed in grief and self-pity that he pushed his two sons away physically and emotionally.[495] Being afraid of his father as a child, C.S. Lewis described his father as a man with "a bad temper, very sensible, nice when not in a bad temper."[496] His father's emotional ups and downs taught Jack a distrust of emotions that would stay with him throughout his life.[497] He called his father's family "true Welshmen, sentimental, passionate, rhetorical" people who moved quickly from laughter to wrath to tenderness, but with no gift for steady contentment.[498]

His father, who dreamed of becoming an MP, instead served as a prosecuting solicitor in the Belfast police court. Swallowed by his work, Jack's father was sometimes cold, remote, distracted, and morose.[499] Albert Lewis had a tendency to cross-examine his sons as if they were on trial.[500] As Jack was so emotionally distant and cutoff from his father, he learned to pretend, avoid and lie to his father to keep him happy.[501] His father, said Jack, "could never empty, or silence, his own mind to make room for an alien thought."[502] His father's life was so orderly one could set a clock by his schedule.[503] When away from his job, he became fidgety and bored, eager to return to his legal responsibilities. Jack was so alienated from his father that he missed how much he was like him. With swift imaginative minds and resounding voices, they both could persuasively make intricate arguments.[504] Jack and his father shared a delightful sense of humour. Albert's sons claimed that he was the best storyteller in the world when he acted out the character parts. His father was very strong on regular church attendance as the right thing to do, but never explained to his sons why.[505] Religion was very private for him.

After ending up in hospital on April 15, 1918 from WWI shrapnel injuries, Lewis wrote his father Albert, saying, "I know that you will come and see me…[I was] never before so eager to cling to every bit of our old home life and see you…Please God, I shall do better in the future. Come and see me." Tragically, his father stayed in Ireland, refusing to change his busy work schedule.[506] Was his father avoiding his unresolved family grief? In October 1918, after successive requests for his father to visit him in hospital, C.S. Lewis wrote his father saying, "It is four months now since I returned from France, and my friends laughingly say that 'my father in Ireland' is a mythical creation."[507]

While still a devout atheist in 1926, C.S. Lewis was attracted by the writings of G.K. Chesterton, especially *The Everlasting Man*. Lewis began to sense that "Christianity itself was very sensible apart from its Christianity." Lewis began to realize that most of the authors he found intellectually nourishing (Spenser, Milton, Johnson, and MacDonald, among others) took 'Christian mythology' seriously while those who 'did not suffer from religion' (Voltaire, Gibbon, Mill, Wells, Shaw) seemed thin and 'tinny' by comparison.[508] He ironically wrote in *Surprised by Joy:* "A young man who wishes to remain a sound atheist cannot be too careful of his reading."[509]

While teaching at Oxford, Jack met J.R.R. Tolkien who persuaded him that Christianity is a true myth, a real story grounded in history.[510] In the summer of 1929, at age thirty, while riding a bus in Oxford, Lewis realized that he was "holding something at bay or shutting something out."[511] He sensed that he was being presented with a free choice, that of opening a door or letting it stay shut. He knew that "to open the door… meant the incalculable."[512] C.S. Lewis went through two conversions, the initial one in 1929 from atheism to theism when he returned to the Anglican Church, and the second one in 1931 to Christ as his personal Lord and Saviour.

Jack's former atheist background helped him reach out to spiritual seekers through books and on the BBC radio. His voice became the most widely recognized in Britain other than Winston Churchill.[513] In 2008, *The Times* ranked him eleventh on their list of "the 50 greatest British writers since 1945."[514]

His books, which still sell six million copies a year, led him to become one of the most influential voices in contemporary Christianity.[515] Gerald Reed observes that, "No other Christian writer's books have been so continuously in print or so widely sold."[516]

The late Chuck Colson, converted by Lewis' book *Mere Christianity*, contended that Lewis is "a true prophet for our post-modern age."[517] As one of the few Christians read extensively by non-Christians, he has become known as the Apostle to the skeptics.[518]

Was it a mere coincidence that C.S. Lewis turned to God in the very summer of his father's death? In August 1929, Lewis went to Belfast to visit his seriously ill father, bringing significant family reconciliation. Albert was glad to have his son with him and seemed surprisingly cheerful, given his condition. Lewis said that his father was taking his surgery "like a hero." A.N. Wilson noted, "All of a sudden, Jack saw that his father was a sort of hero—a maddening, eccentric hero but a man whose decency, courage and good humour were as unshakable as his sincere piety." David Downing commented, "In those few weeks, the elder and younger Lewis found a serenity and closeness in their relationship which they had perhaps not known before."[519]

After his dad's death, Lewis commented, "As times goes on, the thing that emerges is that, whatever else he was, he was a terrific personality…

how he filled a room. How hard it was to realize that physically he was not a big man."[520] Lewis deeply regretted how insensitively he had treated his father.[521]

It was his Narnia tales that ultimately led Joy Davidman, a Jewish atheistic American communist, to become his wife. Their unlikely marriage was initially a marriage of convenience so that she would not be forced to return to the United States. After she initially recovered from cancer, he married her for real. Her later death rocked his clever ideas about life to their core, resulting in the heart-felt book *A Grief Observed*. Once again, he had lost the central female in his life.

How might C.S. Lewis' complicated family life with his dad and wife inspire us to deeper family reconciliation?

Eric Liddell's Fiery Chariots

(1902–1945)

"Suddenly a chariot of fire and horses of fire appeared
and separated the two of them, and Elijah went up to
heaven in a whirlwind." (2nd Kings 2:11, NIV)

Sometimes Eric Liddell ran races against the Japanese guards in order to allow food and medicine to be smuggled in for the starving inmates at the internment camp in China. In one scene of the movie *Wings of Eagles*, Liddell, constantly hungry and weak, is compelled to compete against a brutal Japanese guard. He is so exhausted from the starvation diet that he stumbles and then collapses. Later on, to obtain medication for a dying man, he agrees to run again, winning the race.[522] The only shoes that he had to race with were his worn-out 1924 Olympic running shoes.

How often does a Chinese-born missionary to China become the subject of an Academy Award-winning movie?[523] The people of China see Eric Liddell as their first Olympic gold medalist, even recently unveiling a statue of him.[524] His daughter Patricia Liddell commented, "My father was multi-faceted, he didn't just appeal to religious people. He was born in China, he worked in China, he died in China. He's their Olympic hero." Duncan Hamilton poignantly commented, "In Chinese eyes, he is a true son of their country; he belongs to no one else."[525]

In *Chariots of Fire*, he is shown running for the glory of God in the 1924 Olympics.[526] Eric commented, "I never prayed that I would win a race. I have of course prayed about the athletic meetings, asking that in this too, God might be glorified."[527] A leading sports reporter summed him up as "probably the most illustrious type of muscular Christianity ever known."[528] Nicknamed the *Flying Scotsman*, he famously said: "God made me fast, and when I run, I feel His pleasure."[529] When asked how he ran so quickly, he often said that he ran as fast as he could for the first half of a race, and then asked God to help him run even faster for the second half.[530] Eric won so much gold and silver that his mother hid his trophies under her bed at night, in case of burglary.[531]

Missionary families often make great sacrifices for the sake of the lost. Born in 1902 at Siao Chang on the Great Plain of Northern China, Eric and his older brother Robert were sent in 1912 to the Eltham missionary boarding school in London. While at Eltham, Eric earned the Blackheath Cup as the best athlete of his year, becoming the captain of both the cricket and rugby union teams.[532] Eric did not see his mother again for seven years, nor his father for thirteen years.[533] Since Eric only knew Chinese culture, he experienced enormous culture shock in his parents' homeland of Scotland and at the boarding school in London.

While earning a chemistry degree at the University of Edinburgh, he was not only a track and field runner, but also became an award-winning rugby player for the Scottish national team.[534] Being painfully shy, Eric never could have imagined that he would become the most famous person in Scotland.[535]

Chemistry professor Neil Campbell at Edinburgh commented, "No athlete has ever made a bigger impact on people all around the world, and the description of him as 'the most famous, the most popular, and best-loved athlete Scotland has ever produced' is no exaggeration."[536] Dunky Wright, Scotland's greatest long-distance runner, said of Eric, "he was without doubt the most glorious runner I have ever seen...with such a high moral Christian character."[537]

Eric had a unique running style that coaches tried to cure without success. The *New York Times* noted that he seemed to do everything wrong.[538] The *Daily Mail* sketched him in a cartoon as if he were a rubber contortionist. Throwing his head back, he swayed and rocked like an overloaded express train.[539] Eric was humorously compared to a startled deer, a windmill with its sails off kilter, a terrified ghost, and someone whose joints had never been oiled.[540] Jack Moakley, the wisest and oldest of the American Olympic running team, said, "That lad Liddell's an awful runner, but he's got something. I think he's got what it takes."[541]

It hurt Eric deeply when many called him a traitor for being unwilling to run on Sunday at the Olympics.[542] His strong Christian convictions led him to refuse to work on Sundays, including winning gold medals.

His stunning Olympic win in the 400 metres turned him from a national embarrassment to a celebrated hero.[543] The closest parallel to his new fame was Beatlemania, complete with an actual Eric Liddell fan club.[544]

For Eric, the 1924 Olympics was just a brief diversion on his way to serve as a missionary in China. Before he boarded the boat to China, enormous crowds came to hear him speak in churches. Over a thousand people had to be turned away sometimes because there was no more room.[545]

Eric served in China as a missionary chemistry teacher from 1925 to 1943, first in Tientsin (Tainjin) and later in Siaochan. During a first furlough in 1932, he was ordained as a minister.[546]

In 1941, the fighting between the Chinese and invading Japanese forces became so dangerous that he was forced to send his Canadian wife Florence and their three children back to Canada.[547] Kissing his wife goodbye, he whispered in her ear, "Those who love God never meet for the last time."[548] The Sino-Japan War was often referred to as the 'Forgotten War' because so few foreigners took any interest in it.[549] The Japanese occupiers did not allow Eric to hold church services with any more than ten people present. So, Eric met nine people for afternoon tea, giving out copies of his sermon. These nine people then each met nine other people giving them copies of the sermon until everyone was reached. This became known as the *Afternoon Tea Church*.[550]

The Japanese had sworn that before 1942 had ended, they would grant approval for everyone to leave. On March 12, 1943, the Japanese declared that no 'enemies' would be allowed to leave China. All British and American 'enemies' were to report to Weidendorf Internment Camp, the former Presbyterian Church compound, in the center of Shantung Province, four hundred miles southeast of Tientsin.[551] The Japanese called it a Civilian Assembly Center.[552] Some of the wealthy British business people on the way to the Internment camp brought along beach chairs, silver cutlery, and even a set of golf clubs.[553]

Over one thousand missionaries were imprisoned by the Japanese, many of whom died.[554] In 1943, Eric was sent to the Weixhan Internment Camp in modern-day Weifang, Shandong, with 1800 other prisoners, including one hundred children of missionaries. While interned in this one hundred and fifty by two hundred yard camp, he helped the elderly, taught Bible classes at the camp school, arranged games, and taught science to the children, who referred to him as Uncle Eric.[555] David J. Michell, a child internee, remarked, "He had a smile for everyone."[556] And he was the hardest worker in the internment camp.[557] Sports writer A. A. Thomson said of Eric, "During the worst period of his imprisonment, he was, through his courage and cheerfulness, a tower of strength and sanity to his fellow prisoners."[558]

Influenced by his missionary mentor Dr. E Stanley Jones, Eric wrote a book, *The Disciplines of the Christian Life*.[559] At that time, there was little written material available to instruct Chinese pastors. Eric was passionate about absolute surrender to the will of God.[560] In Eric's 1942 book *Prayers for Daily Use*, he wrote, "Obedience to God's will is the secret of spiritual knowledge and insight. It is not willingness to know but willingness to do (obedience) God's will that brings certainty."[561] His major sermon topics in the internment camp were the Sermon on the Mount and 1 Corinthians 13.[562] In Eric's booklet "The Sermon on the Mount for Sunday School Teachers," he wrote, "Meek is kind and gentle and fearless...Meek is love in the presence of wrong."[563]

One internee said, "He wasn't a very good preacher, but he certainly had us all listening to him because his personality or his sincerity or whatever it was came across so strongly."[564] In a letter to a friend, the Reverend Howard Smith wrote, "I never saw Eric angry. I never heard him say a cross or unkind word. He just went about doing good."[565] Eric was a friend, if you needed him, particularly in times of relationship conflict.[566] A fellow internee said, "Of all the men I have known, Eric Liddell was the one in whose character and life the spirit of Jesus Christ was pre-eminently manifested."[567] He became the camp's conscience without being judgmental or critical of others.[568] He lived his Christianity.[569] Norman Cliff, in his book *Courtyard of the Happy Way*, described Eric as "the most outstanding Weihsien personality...in his early forties, quiet-spoken and with a permanent smile. Eric was the finest Christian man I have had the privilege of meeting."[570]

Eric never saw his family again. Winston Churchill arranged a prisoner swap for Eric Liddell. Amazingly, he gave up this opportunity for freedom to a pregnant woman instead.[571] He died at age forty-three in the internment camp of a brain tumour, just months before the WWII liberation. His last words were, "It's complete surrender."[572]

Langdon Gilkey wrote, "The entire camp, especially its youth, was stunned for days, so great was the vacuum that Eric's death had left."[573] Adopted by the Chinese as their very own, he is commemorated in a monument in Weifang, featuring these words from Isaiah: "They shall mount up with wings as eagles, they shall run and not be weary."[574]

Like Eric Liddell, what might it take for us to feel God's pleasure for the sake of the nations?

Chuck Smith:
Father of the Jesus
Movement Revival

(1927–2013)

"The Spirit and the bride say, 'Come'" (Revelation 22:17, NIV)

Pastor Chuck Smith of Calvary Chapel initially dismissed hippies as parasites upon society,[575] thinking, "Why don't they cut their hair, get a bath and a job?"[576] He wanted nothing to do with them. From Chuck's perspective, "It looked to be a sort of mass regression—as if they'd all willingly regressed to frontier days in appearance and to the magical fairy tales in their thinking."[577] Chuck Smith said to his wife, Kay, "It's too late. They are too far gone. I think they are beyond help."[578] She broke down and started crying, saying, "Chuck, don't say that."

Kay was a deep woman of prayer.[579] She began to think of these homeless youth who roamed the streets as lost children. With growing compassion and curiosity, Chuck and Kay began asking, "Who are they? What do they believe? What kind of relationships do they have with their parents? How did they get so lost?"[580] One day, while visiting Huntington Beach, Kay said to him, "We have to meet a hippie!"[581]

Within a couple of weeks, their future son-in-law brought them a hitch-hiking hippie named Lonnie Frisbee.[582] He looked much like artistic paintings of Jesus.[583] This young hippie had had a profound encounter with Jesus Christ.[584] Chuck said, "With his long hair, beard, and Bohemian clothes, it seemed Lonnie could have easily stepped out of the pages of the Bible. Kay and I were really taken with Lonnie. He had a charismatic presence that came across as gentle and kind, yet firm."[585] Lonnie helped them understand this very strange tribe called hippies. They wanted everyone at Calvary Chapel to meet Lonnie.[586]

The Hippie movement had brought 100,000 youth to Haight-Ashbury in San Francisco for the 1967 Summer of Love.[587] Many became homeless, hungry, and sick.[588] By the end of 1969, many hippies had died from drug overdoses.[589] In December 1969, a young man was stabbed to death at a free rock concert in Altamont, California.[590] Out of the ashes of the failed hippie dream emerged the unexpected Jesus movement.[591]

Through the Jesus movement in the late 1960s and '70s, two to three million young people, including ourselves, came into the Kingdom.[592] Historians now say that the Jesus movement was a full-blown genuine revival that reached more lost people than in the previous Great Awakenings in 1730-1740 and 1790-1840.[593]

Chuck, whom Lonnie called Daddy Chuck, was the dream father figure for thousands of fatherless hippies.[594] Sadly, Lonnie came from a violent, abusive home situation with an alcoholic father who painfully rejected him.[595] After being sexually abused at age eight by his male babysitter, he told his parents this. Refusing to believe him, they tragically sent Lonnie back to his babysitter. It took many years for Lonnie to eventually receive healing for these emotional wounds. Steve Sjogren insightfully commented about Lonnie:

> It seems like there are not enough words in the English language to accurately describe this very unique individual. However, here's a few: brilliant, controversial, gifted off the scale, humble, proud, bold, transparent, teachable, prophetic, friendly, standoffish, childish, worldly, passionate, healed, broken.[596]

Like a spiritual Batman and Robin team, Chuck and Lonnie brought together the Word and the Spirit. Chuck had switched from wanting to be a medical doctor[597] to being a pastor after hearing C. T. Studd's poem at a summer camp: "Only one life, 'twill soon be past, only what's done for Christ will last."[598] He wanted God's will in his life above anything else. Before Lonnie came along, Chuck was close to leaving his tiny congregation. He had a grace-filled anointing for teaching the Bible verse by verse, chapter by chapter.[599] His life theme was connecting people to God's Word: "the spiritual growth that occurred in people was a result of simply reading through the Bible and teaching what God has inspired."[600] Chuck wanted to be remembered "as one who loves the Word of God and the people of God."[601] His genuineness was very attractive to the hippies. Chuck was allergic to spiritual posturing and emotional manipulation.[602]

Rather than shouting for effect, he had a gentle, quieter voice.[603] His infectious smile and delightful sense of humour transcended the deep generation gap.[604] Although he had been through many tragedies and failures, Chuck deeply believed that everything prepared us for something else.[605] Nothing was wasted, not even the painful time when Chuck left the ministry in Corona:

> All I knew then and there was bitter disappointment, failure, and heartache. I understand now that it can be good to sit in failure and come to the end of yourself. Through broken dreams and shattered plans, one learns humility and total dependence on God.[606]

Lonnie was an unusually gifted evangelist who led tens of thousands of hippies into a personal relationship with Jesus Christ.[607] As Lonnie put it, "Nobody thought that a hippie could be saved."[608] Tiny Calvary Chapel soon overflowed with hippies who soiled the church's nice clean carpets and padded pews. A frustrated elder posted a sign, banning people with bare feet and dirty jeans. Pastor Chuck tore the sign down, stating that he would rather rip out the carpets and pews than turn away the hippies.[609] The word on the street was that this was a hippie church with a hippie preacher.[610] When the older conservative-looking Chuck stood up at the pulpit, the hippies initially wondered who had invited him. But he soon won them over with his big heart of love.

Both Chuck and Lonnie were remarkable story-tellers, often weaving the stories of their setbacks and breakthroughs into their gospel presentations. Their humorous transparency was deeply attractive to young hippies who had rejected the plastic pretending of their parents. They both shared a deep love for God's creation. Chuck commented, "God has always used nature to awaken my heart and He has approached me through the wonder of a verdant forest, crystal clear stream, and a stellar jay's scolding more times than I can remember."[611]

"As an artist," Lonnie said, "I cannot put into words how totally in awe I am of God's incredibly beautiful and majestic landscapes…We saw sunrises and sunsets in Africa that literally took my breath away! All creation declares His glory and reality."[612]

The hippies brought the best and sometimes the worst of their counter-culture with them to Calvary Chapel. With every revival comes new music.[613] The Jesus movement birthed what we now think about as Contemporary Christian music.[614] The most famous of the Calvary Chapel bands was LoveSong with Chuck Gerard.[615] Twelve Calvary Chapel bands toured regularly up and down the West Coast.[616] The Jesus Movement music was bigger than just Calvary Chapel. We brought to Vancouver not just Calvary Chapel bands like The Way, but also musicians like Larry Norman, Randy Stonehill, Tom Howard, and Daniel Amos through the LivingStone Productions concert agency.

Everything that Chuck and Lonnie touched turned to spiritual gold, eventually resulting in 1,700 Calvary Chapels in North America and many others overseas. Chuck and Lonnie began baptizing thousands of youth every month at Corona Del Mar Beach.[617] *Time Magazine* and other media turned up, putting Jesus on their front covers.[618] There was a mushrooming of Christian coffeehouses, communes, bumper stickers, films, and Christian newspapers.[619] The most widely read Jesus people newspaper *Right On* (later *Radix*) was produced by The Christian World Liberation Front (later Berkley Christian Coalition).[620] The highly acclaimed *Son-Worshippers* film shared Lonnie's message globally, including to us in our local Winston Churchill High School in Vancouver, BC.[621]

The intense media coverage began to be overwhelming.[622] Lonnie became so busy in the revival that his marriage started to suffer. His wife Connie felt that she was coming a distant third after God and the Church.[623] Lonnie began doing overseas missions with amazing results in terms of young people entering the Kingdom. Sadly, his marriage collapsed, leaving Lonnie very wounded and rejected. Then, Pastor Chuck and Lonnie had a falling out over Lonnie's emphasis on charismatic gifts and healing.

Lonnie received a deeper anointing from his mission outreaches in Africa. Unexpectedly a second outpouring happened on Mother's Day 1980[624], resulting in the birth of a new Vineyard movement with John

Wimber, ultimately resulting in 2,400 Vineyards globally.[625] This brought greater strain between Chuck and Lonnie.[626]

After Lonnie left the Vineyard, he tried to have his own ministry. Sadly, his family wounds left him vulnerable to temptation. Many have compared Lonnie to the biblical Samson.[627] At one point, during great isolation, he fell for a couple of years into a cocaine addiction, and ended up HIV-positive.[628]

In the last few years before Lonnie's death in 1993, he finally got counselling, working on the deep childhood traumas that haunted him.[629] He also worked through the deep father-wound that had left him bitter and angry with other key father figures like Chuck Smith and John Wimber.[630] Deep forgiveness and healing happened in many of those relationships, so much so that Chuck Smith ended up speaking at Lonnie's funeral.[631]

We thank God for Chuck Smith, father of the Jesus Movement, and his spiritual son Lonnie Frisbee whom God used to bring so many of us to Life.[632] May God give us today an even greater revival and awakening than what happened in the Jesus movement.[633]

John Wimber:
God's Risk-Taking Santa Claus

(1934–1997)

"Do not merely listen to the word and so deceive
yourselves. Do what it says." (James 1:22, NIV)

John Wimber came to Christ in 1963 at age twenty-nine as a self-pro-
claimed chain-smoking, beer-guzzling drug abuser.[634] Because his
father abandoned him the day he was born, John didn't know how
to be a good father.[635] His marriage was nearly over.[636] He described
himself as a fourth-generation pagan/unbeliever who had never heard
the gospel.[637] As a gifted entrepreneur, he owned and operated sixty-
one businesses during his sixty-three years on earth.[638] At the top of
his musical career, he played twenty different instruments. John was
the pianist and manager for the Righteous Brothers band (then called
the Paramours) from 1962-1963. After he left the group, the Righteous
Brothers would be the opening act for the Beatles when they were on
their first US tour.

He heard the Lord tell him to give up his musical career. So, he went
from a $100,000 per year to a $7,000 per year as a carpenter's helper,
cleaning out oil tanks.[639] John humorously called this time his purga-
tory: "I was humbled. I used to be pretty mouthy and sure of myself...I
was used to pretty much calling my own shots...God was teaching me
obedience."[640] As rebellion was very deep in John's heart, God never
stopped working on that lesson in his life. John reflected:

> Again, and again, and again, He taught us obedience, obedi-
> ence, obedience, obedience, that he valued obedience above
> all things, and he wanted relationship with us, and he wanted
> our dependence upon Him.[641]

With his gift of the gab, John became a salesman for a collection agency in Los Angeles, California.[642] Everywhere he went, he shared the gospel. People affectionately described him as a cross between Kenny Rogers and Santa Claus.[643] Others saw him as a warm teddy bear.[644] He was relaxed and playful with a winning smile.[645] John, who personally led thousands to Jesus, said that during the Jesus movement, you could sneeze and lead someone to Christ. While trying to fix a leaking water faucet, John had a life-changing vision:

> I looked up at the sky and it was like fire falling, so real to me that I rolled thinking that I don't want it to hit my face. Then suddenly I was in some sort of state where I could see it exploding in the air all across Southern California, and then a fireball going across the ocean, hitting London and exploding over Europe, and then gathering again and going into Asia and Africa...I went to London four times in the 1970s and didn't see any revival.[646]

After becoming an evangelical Quaker pastor at Yorba Linda Friends Church, he soon had the largest Quaker congregation in North America. By 1974, he was approaching burnout, and resigned from pastoral ministry. After his enrolling in the Doctoral program at Fuller Theological Seminary, Dr. Peter Wagner recruited him to be the Founding Director of the Fuller Department of Church Growth. While visiting 2,000 different churches of various denominations, Wimber heard returning missionaries' amazing stories of church growth, miracles and casting out demons.[647] He taught classes for many years at Fuller Seminary, most notably a course in the early 80s called "Signs, Wonders, and Church Growth" which had over 800 registrants, the largest in Fuller's history.[648]

After John Wimber had a Holy Spirit encounter, he was graciously released from the Quakers, and planted Yorba Linda Calvary Chapel in 1977.[649] He had a passion to not just read in the bible about the healing ministry but also to participate in it. John sought to apply George Ladd's theology of the kingdom of God to healing ministry. Ladd taught that the kingdom of God is both present in our midst, but not completely present, already and not yet. For almost a year, Wimber and his congregation prayed for the sick with no one being healed.[650] Many left his congregation. Finally, healings began to take place.[651]

John taught that everyone gets to play, that the work of the Kingdom breaking in is for all Christians, not just for the ordained.[652] He loved to say, "If I can do it, you can do it. Look at me, I'm just a fat man trying to get to heaven."[653] John gave people permission to fail.[654] He never hyped people up, but rather just obeyed the Lord.[655] His willingness to repent was remarkable.[656] He was very gentle and gutsy at the same time.[657] John spelt Faith as R.I.S.K.: "Becoming a disciple is committing yourself to risk-taking the rest of your life, just always having to take chances."[658]

On Mother's Day 1980, he invited Lonnie Frisbee to preach at his church. Lonnie was a key Jesus movement founder with Calvary Chapel. The outpouring of the Holy Spirit that day brought tremendous church growth, and resulted in John becoming the leader of the Vineyard movement in 1982.[659] This did not go over well with Pastor Chuck Smith, founding leader of Calvary Chapel:[660]

The work of the Spirit Smith condoned was relegated to personal spirituality, back rooms and after-service spaces. He firmly avoided up front and public demonstrations and ministry; this, he felt, detracted from the ministry of the Word as central to the worship gathering.[661]

The Vineyards were originally started by Kenn Gulliksen in the homes of Christian musicians Larry Norman and Chuck Girard, which attracted fellow musicians Bob Dylan, Debbie Boone, Priscilla Presley, and Keith Green. It was no wonder that Vineyard music focusing on intimacy with God swept around the world.[662]

Because John believed that church planting is the best form of evangelism, he pioneered the planting of twenty-five hundred Vineyards in North America and in over ninety nations.[663] In the first ten years, the Vineyard grew at a rate of 1100%.[664] Wimber's stated desire as a gifted organizer was to leave a movement behind him like John Wesley did, not just leave converts like George Whitefield. He began leading healing and renewal conferences throughout the world to hundreds of thousands of delegates. Just like with D. L. Moody and Billy Graham, his greatest breakthrough happened in England. John remembered:

When I was invited by (the Reverend Canon) David Watson

to go to London in 1981, I said okay but didn't expect much of it. I had completely forgotten about the (earlier) vision.... When I arrived in London at Gatwick Airport, it was like I had a hand hit my head and knock me flat on my face. As I went down, I heard in my mind "this is that which I have spoken to you about." The next two weeks were incredible.

Bishop David Pytches and Reverend Sandy Millar of Holy Trinity Brompton both commented that John Wimber had a greater impact on the Church of England (Anglican) than anyone since John Wesley.[665] John Wimber modeled his ministry on John Wesley.[666] Bishop David Pytches opened many doors to the Kingdom message that John Wimber was teaching.[667] While John led the Vineyard, he loved the entire Body of Christ.[668]

I (Ed) was privileged to attend a life-changing five-day conference in 1984 with John Wimber with 2,500 other people co-sponsored by Regent College that was held at Burnaby Christian Fellowship. When the Vineyard team individually prayed for me, God once again worked on softening my heart, resulting in experiencing an ocean of God's love.

Sadly, through this rigorous conference speaking, John's health began to suffer. "All my life," Wimber admitted, "I have been a compulsive person, always working and eating more than I should." His travel schedule of more than forty weeks a year gave him a heart attack in 1986. This was followed by sinus cancer in 1993, and a stroke in 1995. Many of us missed John Wimber when he died from a brain hemorrhage in 1997.

Though John is gone, the power of the Holy Spirit to heal and renew is still available for all today who are willing to obediently risk. John taught that a power encounter is only as far away as this prayer: "Holy Spirit, I open my heart, my innermost-being to you. I turn from my sin and self-sufficiency and ask that you fill me with your love, power, and gifts. Come, Holy Spirit."[669]

Dr. J.I. Packer: Knowing God, Longing for the Fire

(1926–2020)

"Therefore, every teacher of the law who has become a disciple in the Kingdom of Heaven is like the owner of a house who brings out of his storeroom new treasures as well as old." (Matthew 13:52, NIV)

W hile chased at age seven by a schoolyard bully, J.I. Packer was struck by a passing bread van, causing a serious head injury which required brain surgery.[670] The medical diagnosis was "a depressed compound fracture of the frontal bone on the right-hand side of his forehead."[671] This brain injury closed the door to his socializing through playing sports. Because of his fragile health, his parents wisely bought him a massive typewriter rather than a bicycle. During his long recovery, the naturally shy Packer read widely, typing his earliest essays. At age seventeen, Packer described himself as a Dostoevsky addict.[672] When asked in his eighties about his strongest childhood memories, he replied, "Solitariness."[673] He was required to wear a black aluminum plate on his head, held in place by an elastic band. At age fifteen, he went on strike, refusing to wear the head plate any longer.[674]

Packer never let his fame and success get to his head. Born on July 22, 1926, he was raised in humble circumstances in the village of Twyning, near Gloucester, in southwest England. McGrath comments about Packer: "Even at an early age, he realized that he was something of a loner, a shy and awkward boy who found it difficult to relate to other children."[675]

Though raised Anglican, Packer did not know Christ personally. While attending Crypt High School, he read C.S. Lewis' *Mere Christianity* and *The Screwtape Letters*.[676] C.S. Lewis' two books, said Packer, "brought me, not indeed to faith in the full sense, but to mainstream

Christian beliefs about God, man, and Jesus Christ, so that I was halfway there."[677] Because of his head injury, Packer was exempted from World War II military service. He became one of the very few who attended Oxford University during that time. On October 22, 1944, while attending an Oxford Christian Union meeting (IVCF), Packer was soundly converted, while singing "Just as I Am": "I had given my life to Christ...When I went out of the church, I knew that I was a Christian."[678] Over fifty years later, he said, "I remember the experience as if it were yesterday."

Over the next few weeks of being discipled, he stopped viewing the Bible as just "a mixed bag of religious all-sorts, of which one could not accept more than the general outlines."[679] Packer commented: "I can still remember the feeling of surprise and gladness, as I left the meeting because I knew that I *knew* that the Bible is the Word of God." Over the next sixty-six years, he took many courageous stands, drawing others back to the Lordship of Jesus and the authority of the Bible. Packer valued tradition and history when seen through the lens of Holy Scripture: Scripture must have the last word on all human attempts to state its meaning, and tradition, viewed as a series of such human attempts, has a ministerial rather than a magisterial role."[680]

Reacting against the 'victorious living' emphasis of the Keswick movement, Packer turned to the spiritual wisdom of the largely forgotten Calvinist Puritans.[681] McGrath observed that "while an older generation looked back on Keswick Conventions for their fellowship and teaching, an emerging generation looked instead to the Puritans."[682] George Whitefield (1714-1770) and the earlier John Owen (1616-1683) became significant mentors in Packer's spiritual maturing.[683] He even did his Oxford doctorate on Richard Baxter, who symbolized the best of the Puritans.[684] Baxter (1615-1691) showed how to be a puritan without being puritanical in the negative sense.[685] Packer's *Knowing God*, published in 1973, is a popularization of his doctoral thesis on Baxter.

Dr. J.I. Packer's unforgettable book *Knowing God* has transformed and revived the hearts and minds of millions of readers.[686] *Christianity Today* readers named him one of the most influential theological writers of the last hundred years, second only to C.S. Lewis.[687] Dr. Alister McGrath called him a theological and spiritual giant:[688] "Packer is a rare example of an original thinker with a genuine gift for teaching."[689] His legacy includes thirty books and over three hundred major articles.[690] Timothy George commented that "his writings are so voluminous that it is hard to imagine that they have come from the pen of one person."[691]

Knowing God was originally written as a series of articles for the UK-based *Evangelical Magazine.* Packer said, "I wrote *Knowing God* over a period of years during which I was deeply concerned, as I still am, to help people realize God's greatness."[692] Intervarsity Press UK (IVP) passed up the chance to publish it, because they wanted Packer instead to write a book about charismatic renewal. Hodder and Stoughton UK initially published it instead. It was in North America, however, that *Knowing God* would have its greatest impact, where IVP USA published it.[693] McGrath said that Packer's personal opinion was that the book succeeded because it allowed its readers to find and experience the reality of God.[694] Best-selling author Dr. John R. W. Stott reviewed *Knowing God,* saying, "The truth he handles fires the heart. At least it fired mine, and compelled me to turn aside to worship and to pray."[695] Dr. Alister McGrath commented that reading *Knowing God* "is like going on a long walk along a forest trail, rich in flora and fauna, nestling under the shadow of the great Rocky Mountains."[696]

McGrath commented that Packer "greatly admired the preaching of Martyn Lloyd-Jones, particularly its expository thoroughness."[697] Through the influence of Lloyd-Jones, Packer developed a passion for revival. In 1949, Packer and Lloyd-Jones birthed the very influential Puritan Conferences, which continued at Westminster Chapel in London until 1970.[698] McGrath commented:

> [The Puritan Studies Conference] offered a powerful and persuasive vision of the Christian life, in which theology, biblical exposition, spirituality and preaching were shown to be mutually indispensable and interrelated. It was a vision of the Christian life which possessed both intellectual rigour and pastoral relevance. It was a powerful antidote to the anti-intellectualism which had been rampant within British evangelical circles in the immediate post-war period.[699]

In the foreword to Lloyd-Jones' *Revival* book, Packer said, "No concern was dearer to his heart nor to mine."[700] Packer observed, "Dr Lloyd-Jones hoped for revival until he died. He is gone. The prophets are gone, but we should still be hoping for revival. Revival is a sovereign work of God. He fixes the time table. The schedule is his, not ours." As Calvinist puritans, both Lloyd-Jones and Packer taught that revival is a sovereign act of God.[701] We cannot produce it through our organizational skills.[702]

Before moving to Vancouver's Regent College in 1979, Packer taught in several English theological settings including Oak Hill College, St. John's Birmingham, Latimer House, Tyndale Hall, and Trinity College Bristol.[703] The pull of North America became stronger after Packer began lecturing during the summers in USA and Canada.[704] As McGrath put it, Packer liked Vancouver, and he liked Canada, which seemed to him to be halfway between Britain and the United States.[705] Regent offered Packer a much greater opportunity to write and to speak at North American conferences.[706] Leland Ryken noted that there has been no more famous teacher at Regent College through the years than Packer.[707] During Packer's time at Regent, the student body grew from one hundred and forty students to over eight hundred.[708]

Charles Colson, founder of Prison Fellowship, stated that "this will be known as the Packer Era because J.I. Packer has been the towering figure of this era—defending truth, defending orthodoxy, and defending great preaching."[709] In 1994, Packer was the chief architect of the Anglican Essentials movement in Canada which ultimately realigned many with the revival in the Global South.[710] The Montreal Essential Declaration is shaped by Richard Baxter's maxim "In essentials, unity; In non-essentials, diversity, and in all things charity."[711] In 2000, he chaired the theological track at the World Conference on Evangelism convened by Billy Graham in Amsterdam.[712] He served for many years as general editor in producing the 2001 *English Standard Version* Bible.[713] Packer had a passion for the revival of catechism, for teaching how to live out biblical truth.[714] Revival, said Packer, means "power, constant sustained power from God's Holy Spirit for life and service."[715] Revival means struggle for truth.[716] Revival is about knowing God.[717]

What might it take for us, like J.I. Packer, to long for the fire of revival?

Conclusion

H as your heart been quickened as you have learned more about God's Firestarters and their families?

You are not alone in your hunger for awakening and revival. God is saying "Awake my soul! Awake, harp and lyre! I will awaken the dawn." (Psalm 57:8) Has your longing deepened for a fresh visitation of the Holy Spirit in this challenging season? How desperate are you to hear God speak from heaven, forgive our sins, and heal our land? We stand at a critical crossroad, and forces are constantly at work to undermine the very moral fabric of our families, churches and nations. We are on the edge of a precipice that many people refuse to see, but it is very real.

God wants you to claim your revival inheritance before it is too late. Repent and turn from your self-absorption, and He will have mercy upon you and on your children's children. Now is the hour! Now is the time! Now is the day of salvation. Let us not be found wanting.

Have your ears been opened? Do you hear God's trumpet call to once again pick up the torch of revival? A new day is dawning. Can you hear the sound of abundant rain? As God said in Zechariah 4:6-7, this revival will happen not by might, nor by power, but by my Spirit. Don't let your hands hang limp any longer in cynicism and despair. God is saying to us in the words of Ephesians 5:14, "awake o sleeper, rise from the dead, and Christ will shine on you." Jesus loves you and your family with an everlasting love.

Will you and your families join us in humbling themselves, praying, seeking His face, and turning from our wicked ways? Are you willing to battle for the soul of your family, your nation, and indeed of planet earth? We urgently need a fresh touch from Jesus' almighty hand. Please join us in trusting God in these dark times for coming revival, refreshing, renewal, and awakening. God is on the move. He will not fail us. May the Lord prayerfully prepare our families for upcoming revivals.

Bend us, Lord. We surrender. Empty us of sin. Cleanse us with your blood. Wake us up. Fill us with your Holy Spirit. Send the fire once again. Revive us, transform us, renew us, refresh us, in Jesus' name. Amen.

Twenty Discussion Questions for Twenty Firestarters

1) Katharina Luther: Reformation Fire Starter
   -In what ways did Katharina's contributions and giftings help bring revival and family reformation?

2) Richard and Margaret Baxter: The Puritan Fire of Love
   -What has been the lasting revival impact of Richard & Margaret's Christ-centered romance?

3) Susanna Wesley: Mother on Fire
   -In what ways did Susanna help prepare her family for the revival fires in the First Great Awakening?

4) John and Charles Wesley: Hearts Strangely Warmed
   -How did God use failure and setback to prepare the Wesley brothers for unexpected revival?

5) George Whitefield: Awakening to the Fire of Christ
   -How did God use Whitefield and the First Great Awakening to birth the U.S.A.?

6) John and Mary Newton: From slavery to freedom fire
   -How did God use the unlikely Newtons to bring lasting freedom for the slaves?

7) William Carey: Fire Starter for World Missions
   -In what ways did Carey release a new passion for world missions?

8) Dr. Livingstone, I Presume: Setting Africa on Fire with the Father's Love
   -Why do Africans remember Dr. Livingstone so fondly in contrast to many other explorers?

9) General William and Catherine Booth: The Fire and the Blood
   -How did the marriage of William and Catherine help release the Fire and the Blood?

10) A.B. Simpson: A Canadian Firestarter for the Nations
    -In what ways has Simpson's four-fold gospel emphasis helped bring revival to the nations?

11) John G. Lake and the Healing Rooms revival
    -Why do you think that the healing rooms revival has struck such a chord with our current culture?

12) Evan Roberts: In the Fiery Land of Revivals
    -Where does God want to bend you in preparation for coming revivals?

13) Dr. E. Stanley Jones: Global Firestarter
    -Why do you think that God gave Jones such favour with Mahatma Gandhi?

14) Aimee Semple McPherson: God's Dynamo
    -What can we learn today from Aimee's four-square gospel emphasis as we prepare for coming revivals?

15) Corrie Ten Boom: Impact Through Fiery Surrender
    -How does God use forgiveness in revivals? Whom do you need to forgive?

16) C.S. Lewis: Surprised by the Fire
    -Why does the renewal of the mind matter in times of revival?

17) Eric Liddell: Fiery Chariots
    -How did God use Liddell's suffering to help bring revival in China?

18) Chuck Smith: Father of the Jesus Movement Revival
    -How might the 1970's Jesus Movement help us prepare for coming greater revivals?

19) John Wimber: God's Risk-Taking Santa Claus
    -How did the life of John Wimber inspire us to trust God for the impossible in future revivals?

20) Dr. J.I. Packer: Knowing God, Longing for the Fire
    -Why have many people underestimated how much Dr. Packer longed for revival? How might we learn from Packer's revival passion?

Endnotes

1 Rudolf K. Markwald and Marilyn Morris Markwald, *Katharina von Bora: A Reformation Life* (St. Louis, MO: Concordia Publishing House, 2002), 46.

2 Ruth A. Tucker, *Katie Luther, First Lady of the Reformation* (Grand Rapids, MI: Zondervan, 2017), 47.

3 Ibid, 49.

4 Ibid, 17.

5 Ibid, 17.

6 Markwald & Markwald, *Katharina von Bora*, 43, "[N]o vow is valid unless it has been made willingly and with love."

7 Ibid, 76.

8 Ibid, 79.

9 Ibid, 79.

10 Tucker, Katie Luther, 79, quoting Luther: "I hope to live a short while yet, to gratify my father, who asked me to marry and leave him descendants...God has caused and willed my act, for I neither love my wife nor burn for her, but esteem her highly."

11 In Eastern Orthodoxy, clergy were allowed to become married prior to their being priested. Once priested, they must remain single, but can stay married if already married. Bishops in Eastern Orthodoxy, however, must be single. "Marriage and Orthodox Priests", First Things, November 2015, https://www.firstthings.com/web-exclusives/2015/10/of-marriage-and-orthodox-priests (accessed June 14th 2021).

12 Marjorie Elizabeth Plummer, *From Priest's Whore to Pastor's Wife* (Surrey, UK: Ashgate Publishing Limited, 2012). This is the most definitive book that we have read on the transition to legal marriage for Western clergy. It shows that whether one was married or not to one's former housekeeper was the measurement of whether one was counted as Protestant clergy rather than a Catholic priest.

13 Minneapolis Museum of Art and The Morgan Library and Museum, *Martin Luther: Treasures of the Reformation,* (Dresden, Germany: Sandstein Verlag, 2004), 219.

14 Tucker, *Katie Luther,* 78.

15 Ernest Kroker, *The Mother of the Reformation: The Amazing Life and Story of Katharine Luther* (St Louis, MO: Concordia Publishing House, 2013), 73.

16 Tucker, *Katie Luther,* 9.

17 William Lazareth, *Luther on the Christian Home* (Philadelphia, PA, Mulenberg, 1960), 23; Tucker, *Katie Luther,* 61.

18 Tucker, *Katie Luther,* 163.

19 Jaroslav Pelikan and Helmut T. Lehman, eds., *Luther's Works* (Philadelphia, PA and St. Louis, MO: Muehlenberg and Fortress, and Concordia, 1955-86), 54:191

20 Martin Brecht, *Martin Luther: Shaping & Defining the Reformation* (Minneapolis, MN: Fortress Press, 1990), 202-203; Robert Dean Linder, *The Reformation Era* (Westport, CT: Greenwood, 2008), 26.; Tucker, *Katie Luther,* 81, 85, "The straw in Luther's bed had not been aired...for a year, so that it was rotting from the moisture of his sweat."

21 Tucker, *Katie Luther,* 121.

22 Heinz Schilling, *Martin Luther: Rebel in An Age of Upheaval,* trans. Rona Johnson (Oxford, UK: Oxford University Press, 2017) 283

23 Tucker, *Katie Luther,* "What she (Katie) probably had not realized before they were married was how entirely inept her new husband was in financial matters...He pawned some of their wedding presents but even then the debt was only half paid. He was paid nothing for his preaching" (p. 85).

24 Ibid, 121, "[T]there were at times as many as thirty students boarding at the Black Cloister, paying for their keep in varying degrees."

25 Ibid, 145.

26 Paul Thigpen, "Martin Luther's Later Years: A Gallery—Family Album: Katherine Von Bora (1499–1552), Runaway Nun Who Became Luther's 'Lord,' " *Christian History* 39 (1993): https://christianhistoryinstitute.org/magazine/article/martin-luthers-gallery-family-album/.

27 Tucker, *Katie Luther,* 123.

28 Ibid, 122;.

29 Markwald & Markwald, *Katharina von Bora,* 82.

30 Ibid, 123.

31 Rick Steves, "Rick Steves' Luther and the Reformation," August 23, 2017, Simon Griffith, 56:00, https://www.amazon.com/Rick-Steves-Luther-Reformation/dp/B07957CN4F.

32 Tucker, *Katie Luther,* 92.

33 Ibid, 124.

34 Ibid, 130.

35 Ibid, 130.

36 The Black Plague started slowly at first, but by May of 1665, 43 people had died. In June 6,137 people died. In July, 17,036 people died, and at its peak in August, 31,159 people died. "History of England, The Great Plague", https://www.historic-uk.com/HistoryUK/HistoryofEngland/The-Great-Plague/ (accessed June 14th 2021).

37 Jonathan Williams, "What Can the COVID-19 Generation Learn from the Great Plague Generation?" Gospel Family (blog), March 19,2020, www.gospelfamily.org/blog/what-can-the-covid-19-generation-learn-from-the-great-plague-generation.

38 J.I. Packer, *A Grief Sanctified: Passing through Grief to Peace and Joy* (Ann Arbor, MI: Vine Books, Servant Publications, 1997), 22. Margaret and her mother Mrs. Hanmer followed Pastor Richard Baxter in April 1660 to London where he was involved in the forthcoming restoration of the Church of England. In 1661, Mrs Hanmer died of fever. On April 29, 1662, after Richard's ejection from the Church of England, he received a license to marry Margaret. After "many changes…stoppages…and long delays," they married on September 10, 1662.

39 Ibid, 115.

40 Ibid, 116.

41 Ibid, *19.*

42 Ibid, 97. Baxter commented: "[H]er mother's house, being a garrison, it was stormed when she was in it, and part of the housing about it burnt, and men lay killed before her face. And all of them were threatened and stripped of their clothing so that they were obliged to borrow clothes."

43 Ibid, 126. Baxter wrote about "[F]our times in danger of death, and the storming of her mother's house by soldiers, firing part, killing, plundering, and threatening the rest."

44 Ibid, 100. Baxter commented that "the unsuitableness of our age, and my former known purposes against marriage, and against the conveniency of minister's marriage, who have no sort of necessity, made our marriage the matter of much public talk and wonder."

45 Ibid, 43.

46 Hugh Martin, *Puritanism and Richard Baxter* (London, UK: SCM Press, 1954), 55, "On Sunday August 17th 1662, some 2,000 ministers took farewell of their parishes, often in the presence of overflowing and weeping congregations. One in five of the clergy were ejected." Martin, 125, "Richard Baxter is usually credited with 168 books."

47 Packer, *A Grief Sanctified,* 44, "[W]herever Richard was and whatever he was doing, he was the object of continual spying and sniping; he was the tall poppy among Puritan nonconformists."

48 Ibid, 20, "Kidderminster was an artisan community of some eighteen hundred adults, with weaving as its cottage industry. Half the town crowded into church every Sunday, and many hundreds had professed conversion."

49 Ibid, 13.

50 Ibid, 15. "Mere Christianity" —meaning historic mainstream Bible-based discipleship to Jesus Christ, without extras, omissions, diminutions, disproportions, or distortions—was

Baxter's own phrase for the faith he held and sought to spread. Three centuries after his time, C.S. Lewis used the same phrase as a title for his 1952 book in which he put together three sets of broadcast talks on Christian basics. Lewis probably got the phrase from Baxter. "Lewis and Baxter belong together as men with a common purpose as well as a common faith. Now Lewis, like Baxter, also lost his wife in his sixties, and while in the grip of grief, turned to writing—the end product being his justly admired *A Grief Observed.*"

51 Ibid, 19, "That means they were gloomy, censorious English Pharisees, who wore black clothes and steeple hats, condemned all cheerfulness, hated the British monarchy, and wanted the Church of England and its Book of Common Prayer abolished—right? Wrong—off track on every point!"

52 Ibid, 23.

53 Ibid, 53. "Richard Baxter was a communicative man, the kind of magnetic, commanding person who makes you feel that he is taking you into his confidence every time he opens his mouth or puts pen to paper. Augustine, C.S. Lewis, and Billy Graham are four more instances of this human type—all of them, incidentally, persons with whom in different ways, Baxter is comparable."

54 Richard Baxter, *The Saints' Everlasting Rest* (Christian Classics Ethereal Library, 1652), 153, http://www.ccel.org/ccel/baxter/saints_rest.html; J.I. Packer, "Morning Devotions Talk," AMiA Winter Conference 2010, Greensboro, NC. This integration of heart and head in knowing God is a strong emphasis by Dr J.I. Packer as he warns against "hardness of heart and cynicism of the head."

55 Packer, *A Grief Sanctified,* back cover, "A True Love Story. Richard and Margaret Baxter came from landowning families who formed England's aristocracy in the 1600s. Richard was a Puritan evangelist, pastor and tireless author. When Richard met Margaret, she was a frivolous, world-minded teenager."

56 Ibid, 119.

57 Michael A. G. Haykin, "Margaret Charlton Baxter: A Puritan Wife," *Bede's Wall, The Gospel Coalition,* September 25, 2017, https://ca.thegospelcoalition.org/columns/bedes-wall/margaret-charlton-baxter-puritan-wife/, "Initially, when Margaret heard Baxter's preaching, she had little liking for either him or the people of the town. She had, Baxter tells us in his life of Margaret—A Breviate of the Life of Margaret…Charlton—a 'great aversion to the poverty and strictness of the people' of the town. Frivolous and held by the gaieties of this world, she was far more interested in 'glittering herself in costly apparel.'"

58 Packer, *A Grief Sanctified,* 22. "[S]he sickened, and for months seemed to be mortally ill with lung problems that nothing would relieve. Special intercession with fasting for her life by Baxter and his inner circle of prayer warriors resulted, however, in a sudden cure 'as if it were nothing'—a healing which today would be called miraculous, and was one of several such in Kidderminster in Baxter's time."

59 Ibid, 64-65.

60 Ibid, 102.

61 Ibid, 119. Baxter commented that "she was for universal love of all true Christians, and against appropriating the Church to a party, and against censoriousness and partiality in religion…" Ibid, 124. Baxter said: "But no one was ever readier (than Margaret) to forgive a fault confessed, and which weakness and religious differences caused."

62 Ibid, 187. Baxter wrote: "For though she often said that before she married me, she expected more sourness and unsuitableness than she found; yet I am sure that she found less zeal and holiness and strictness in all words and looks and duties, and less help for her soul, than she expected."

63 Ibid, 110. Baxter commented that "so much was her heart set on the helping the ignorant, untaught poor about St. James' that she set up a school there to teach some poor children to read, and the catechism, freely."

64 Ibid, 106, 108. Baxter commented that "the place being greatly crowded, the beam gave so great a crack as put all the people in a fear. But a second crack set them all on running and crying out at the windows for ladders… After the first crack, she got down the stairs through the crowd, where others could not get that were stronger. The first man she met, she asked him what profession he was of? He said, a carpenter. Saith she, 'Can you suddenly put a prop under the middle of this beam?' The man dwelt close by and had a meet prop ready. He suddenly put it under, while all we above knew nothing of it; but the man's knocking increased the people's fears and cry."

65 Ibid, 108. Baxter commented: "But this fright increased my wife's diseased frightfulness… And if eight hundred persons had been buried in the ruins, as the Papists were in Blackfriars, O what a dreadful thing it would have been in the heavy loss, the many dolorous families, and the public scandal!"

66 Ibid, 126. Baxter wrote that "[S]he could not bear the clapping of a door or anything that had suddenness, noise or fierceness in it. [She]…was more fearless of persecution, imprisonment, or losses and poverty thereby, than I or any that I remember to have known."

67 Ibid, 113. Baxter commented, "When warrants were out [from Sir Thomas Davis] to distrain of [i.e., confiscate and sell] my goods for fines for my preaching, she did without any repining encourage me to undergo the loss and did herself take the trouble of removing and hiding my library awhile (many score books being so lost), and after she encouraged me to give it away, bona fide, some to New England, and the most at home to avoid distraining on them. And the danger of imprisonment and of paying a fine of 40 pounds for every sermon."

68 Ibid, 47. On the occasion when Baxter's home preaching landed him in Clerkenwell jail with a six-month sentence, she "cheerfully went with me into prison; she brought her best bed thither… I think she scarce ever had a pleasanter time in her life"; Mylordkatie, "Margaret Baxter: A High Calling," My Lord Katie: Educating, Inspiring, and Motivating Christian Women (blog), June 21, 2012, https://mylordkatie.wordpress.com/2012/06/21/margaret-baxter-a-high-calling/, "So completely loyal was Margaret that she insisted on joining him in prison! A friendly jailor allowed her to make the prison room comfortable for Richard and herself."

69 Packer, A Grief Sanctified, 47, 104.

70 Ibid, 186, "Richard and Margaret, the workaholic pastor and the willful rich girl, started with the Puritan idea of marriage and built their relationship on that basis with spectacular success. As we can now see, they loved each other realistically, neither idolizing nor idealizing each other."

71 Ibid, 186.

72 Ibid, 44, 146. Baxter commented, "The pleasing of a wife is usually no easy task. There is an unsuitableness in the best and wisest and most alike… Those who agree in religion, in love and interest, yet may have different apprehensions about occasional occurrences, persons, things, words. That will seem the best way to one that seems the worst to the other. And passions are apt to succeed and serve these differences. Very good people are hard to be pleased. My own dear wife had high desires of my doing and speaking better than I did, but my badness made it hard for me to do better." "My dear wife did look for more good in me than she found, especially lately in my weakness and decay. We are all like pictures that must not be looked up too near. Those that come near us find more faults and badness in us than others at a distance know."

73 Ibid, 97; 117, "Richard celebrates Margaret's quick intelligence, competence in business, brilliance with moral dilemmas, joy in the gospel, in God, in godliness and in being a despised nonconformist, excellence as a homemaker, gentle patience with people of all sorts, faithfulness in chiding her husband as necessary, desire for fullest spiritual intimacy with him at all times. And great love for her mother, despite battles with nightmarish fears that threatened her sanity."

74 Ibid, 60, "I had been bred among plain, lower-class people, and I thought that so much washing of stairs and rooms, to keep them as clean as possible their trenches and dishes, and so much ado about cleanliness and trifles, was a sinful eccentricity and expense of servants' time, while have been spent reading a good book. But she that had otherwise been bred had somewhat other thoughts."

75 Ibid, 31, "See that you be furnished with marriage strength and patience, for the duties and sufferings of a married state, before you venture on it."

76 Ibid, 13, "Debarred in 1662 from parochial ministry by the unacceptable terms on which the Act of Uniformity reestablished the Church of England, he made writing his main business".

77 Martin, *Puritanism and Richard Baxter*, 176, 180. Baxter inspired Wilberforce by his fearless stand against the slave trade, saying: "To go as pirates and catch up poor negroes or people of another land, that never forfeited life or liberty, and to make them slaves, and sell them, is one of the worse kinds of thievery in the world;" "Richard Boyce the scientist said that Richard Baxter feared no man's displeasure, nor hoped for any man's preferment."

78 Ibid, 125, "Baxter's influence of the 'Clapham Sect' is just one part of the story of his speaking after death"; 131, "(Baxter's) 'Reformed Pastor' influenced Spener, the founder of German Pietism"; 146, "Spurgeon (was a) close student of the Puritan preachers, including Baxter."; J.I. Packer, *A Quest for Godliness: The Puritan Vision of the Christian Life* (Wheaton, IL: Crossway Books, 1994).

79 Packer, *A Grief Sanctified*, 123.

80 Ibid, 45, 121. Baxter commented: "She was very desirous that we should all have lived in a constancy of devotion and a blameless innocency. And in this respect, she was the meetest helper that I could have had in the world… for I was apt to be over-careless in my speech and too backward to my duty, and she was always endeavoring to bring me to greater wariness and strictness in both. If I spoke rashly or sharply, it offended her; if I behaved (as I was apt) with too much neglect of ceremony or humble compliment to any, she would modestly tell me of it; if my very looks seemed not pleasant, she would have me amend them (which my weak, pained state of body undisposed me to do); if I forgot any week to catechize my servants and familiarly instruct them personally (beside my ordinary family duties [i.e. household prayers twice daily]), she was troubled at my remissiveness."

81 Ibid, 99. Baxter commented that "[H]er fervent, secret prayers; for, living in a great house of which the middle part was ruined by the [Civil] wars, she chose a closet in the further end, where she thought none heard it. But some who overheard her said they never heard so fervent prayers from any person."

82 Ibid, 120.

83 Ibid, 46. "It was not the least comfort that I had in the converse of my late dear wife, that our first in the morning and last in bed at night was a psalm of praise."

84 Ibid, 44.

85 Ibid, 123. Baxter commented: "She could not well bear to hear one speak loud or hastily or eagerly or angrily, even to those who deserved it. My temper in this she blamed as too quick and earnest."

86 Ibid, 44. "Moreover, neither of them had a really easy temperament. Margaret was highly strung and a bundle of fears inside, which she made worse by bottling them up; Richard was hasty and frequently offhand, as persons who live in pain often are, and was inclined to be downcast and irritable when things did not go his way."

87 Ibid, 47. "She was obsessive about her health, too, spending much of her adult life in fear of mental collapse, starving herself for years for fear that overeating would bring on cancer, and thereby as it seems undermining her own constitution."

88 Ibid, 43, 103. Baxter commented that "[S]he could not endure to hear one give another any sour, rough, or hasty word. Her speech was always kind and civil, whether she had anything to give or not."

89 Ibid, 171, "Richard, who had thought of himself from the age of twenty as living with one foot in the grave"; 149, Baxter finished his book on Margaret with these words: "I am waiting to be next. The door is open. Death will quickly draw the veil and make us see how near we were to God and one another, and did not sufficiently know it. Farewell vain world, and welcome true everlasting life. Finis."

90 Ibid, 53.

91 Ibid, 97. Baxter commented: "She was of an extraordinary sharp and piercing wit. She had a natural reservedness and secrecy, increased by thinking it necessary prudence not to be open…she had a natural tenderness and troubledness of mind upon the crossing of her just desires…she had a diseased, unresistable fearfulness; her quick and too sensitive nature was over-timorous"; 120, Baxter commented, "If I spoke rashly or sharply, it offended her."

92 Ibid, 127. Baxter commented: "Indeed, she was so much for calmness, deliberation, and doing nothing rashly and in haste, and my condition and business as well as temper made me do and speak much so suddenly, that she principally differed from me and blamed me in this: Every considerable case and business she would have me take time to think much of before I did it or spoke or resolved of anything";127-128, Baxter commented, "[N]ot withstanding her over-quick and feeling temper, was all for mildness, calmness, gentleness, pleasingness, and serenity."

93 Ibid, 45, 170; Lloyd-Thomas, 249.

94 Packer, A Grief Sanctified, 118. Baxter commented, "Yes, I will say that, except in cases that required learning and skill in theological difficulties, she was better at resolving a case of conscience than most divines that ever I knew in all my life."

95 Mylordkatie, "Margaret Baxter," "Finally, the doctors followed the common practice of bleeding her and she lost the last of her strength. After severe illness for twelve days, she died on June 14, 1681, aged only forty-two."

96 Packer, A Grief Sanctified, 13.

97 Ibid, 15, "Baxter's Breviate, though low-key and matter-of-fact in style, is Puritan spiritual storytelling at its best: story telling that is made more poignant by Richard's intermittent unveiling of his grief as he goes along.

98 Ibid, 177.

99 Ibid, 162 "Richard and Lewis each gave the world a small book forged in the furnace of grief that is frank, poignant, profound, and a lifeline for the bereaved."

100 Ibid, 164. Packer commented that, "In our death-denying, live-forever-down-here culture, we do not know how to cope with the emotional effect of our loved one's death."

101 Ibid, 181, "Popular culture today treats structure in relationships as restrictive rather than liberating, and impoverishing than enriching"; 193, "For Richard and Margaret, as for the whole Bible-based Puritan movement, marriage was a covenant partnership meant to be God-centered and lifelong, a privilege, a calling, and a task."

102 Ibid, 31, "Richard brings all this down to earth, stressing that what makes for God-honoring marriage is not euphoria but character, consideration, and commitment: in other words, personal formation, reflection, and resolution."

103 Ibid, 30.

104 Ibid, 181. Baxter commented, "You see here that suitableness in religious judgement and disposition preserveth faster love and concord (as it did with us) than suitableness in age, education, and wealth… Nothing causest so near and fast and comfortable a union as to be united in one God, one Christ, one Spirit, one church, one hope of heavenly glory"; 189, "[T]he experiential emotional fruit of the bereavement event, is, as we have seen, a state of desolation and isolation, of alternating apathy and agony, of inner emptiness and exhaustion… Do not let your grief loosen your grip on the goodness and grace of your loving Lord."

105 Ibid, 167, "Richard, whose memoir praises God for Margaret, and Margaret herself for her godliness, throughout"; 171, "Richard's sense of deserving none of the good gifts of earthly marriage."

106 Ibid, 177. "Richard's purpose of writing 'true history' led him to recount Margaret's weaknesses, flaws, and struggles alongside her strengths, virtues, and achievements. He does not present as a plaster saint but as a born-again servant of God with a heart of gold, feet of clay, and huge natural vulnerabilities."

107 Ibid, 193. "Why did I put this book together? … First I wanted you to meet Richard Baxter. Through his writings, he has been a close personal friend of mine for over half a century, and I wanted to share him. An outstanding pastoral evangelist, a gifted and prolific devotional writer, and a major prophet (unheeded, unfortunately) to the Anglican Church in the second half of the seventeenth century, he is endlessly interesting; for beyond his public roles he was a great and communicative human being who lets you hear his heart beat as he writes… I wanted to introduce you to him as a husband working at his Puritan marriage, and as a widower grieving for the lively lady who had been his life-partner for almost twenty years… They were two memorable Christian people with whom I would have loved to spend time… They enrich my life; I should like them to enrich yours too."

108 EpworthOldRectory, "Susanna's Influence," July 30, 2012, YouTube, 2:59, https://www.youtube.com/watch?v=VgaKxoBAUZ4; Eric Metaxas, *Seven Women and the Secret of their Greatness* (Nashville, TN: Nelson Books, 2015), 41.

109 Charles Ludwig, *Susanna Wesley: Mother of John and Charles* (Milford, MI: Mott Media, 1984), 150; PastorStudy, "Susanna Wesley and the High Calling of Christian Parenthood," December 14, 2014, YouTube, 28:30, https://www.youtube.com/watch?v=7yj23etRkGU. Her son Charles produced over 3,000 hymns.

110 Edith Deen, *Great Women of the Christian Faith*, (Chappaqua, NY: Christian Herald Books, 1959), 141.

111 Ibid, 144.

112 Ludwig, *Susanna Wesley*, Inside page.

113 Jean Miller Schmidt, *Grace Sufficient: A History of Women in Early Methodism 1760-1939*, (Nashville, TN: Abingdon Press, 1999), 25; Frank Baker, "Susanna Wesley: Puritan, Parent, Pastor, Protagonist, Pattern," in *Women in New Worlds: Historical Perspectives on the Wesleyan Tradition*, ed. Rosemary Skinner Keller, Louise L. Queen, and Hilah Frances Thomas, (Nashville, TN: Abingdon Press, 1981), 2:112-131.

114 United Methodist Videos, "Susanna Wesley: Mother of Methodism," April 7, 2016, YouTube, 3:50, https://www.youtube.com/watch?v=Zpi1OJ5LiVY. Susanna is the mother of one of history's dynamic duos. John and Charles Wesley are their mother's sons. She is the person responsible for their education and spiritual formation.

115 "…Susanna by whom he was prayerfully educated in the things of God" (plaque in the modern Epworth Methodist Church).

116 Eric Metaxas, *Seven Women*, 38.

117 Ibid, 37, "It was not at all customary to educate girls at that time, so it is remarkable that Susanna wanted not just her three sons, but all her children to be able to read, write and reason well."

118 Ibid, 39.

119 Ibid, 38.

120 Ibid, 38.

121 Ludwig, *Susanna Wesley*, 118, "Sam's debts worried Susanna. And she was concerned about his carelessness with money."

122 Metaxas, *Seven Women*, 37. The last five children were born after Samuel and Susanna reconciled.

123 Ruth A. Tucker, *First Ladies of the Parish: Historical Portraits of Pastors' Wives* (Grand Rapids, MI: Zondervan Publishing House, 1988) 53.

124 Metaxas, *Seven Women*, 37.

125 Ludwig, *Susanna Wesley*, 164.; Tucker, First Ladies of the Parish, 53 "[T]hey…pried the hinges off the rectory doors…once even tried to cut off the legs of the house dog."

126 Ludwig, *Susanna Wesley*, 130.; Metaxas, *Seven Women*, 41-42.

127 Deji Okegbile, "John Wesley, 310 Years After: "A Brand Plucked Out of the Fire," The Deji Okegbile Blog, February 28, 2019, http://dejiokegbile.com/ john-wesley-310-years-after-a-brand-plucked-out-of-the-fire/.

128 Tucker, *First Ladies of the Parish*, 56.

129 Tucker, *Firs Ladies of the Parish*, 55 -56.; Deen, *Great Women*, 146.

130 Deen, *Great Women*, 146. "It was his mother Susanna who sent him a letter of encouragement: 'I was much pleased with your letter to your father about taking holy orders and liked the proposal. I approve your decision and think the sooner you are a deacon, the better.'"

131 Ibid, 147.

132 Ibid, 148.

133 Metaxas, *Seven Women*, 54.

134 Ibid, 56. Twelve hours before her death, she awoke and prayed: "My dear Saviour! Are you come to help me in my extremity at last?"

135 United Methodist Church, "John Wesley's American Parish," General Commission on Archives and History, 2021, http://www.gcah.org/research/travelers-guide/ john-wesleys-american-parish.

136 "The Moravians and John Wesley," *Christianity Today Magazine*, https://www. christianitytoday.com/history/issues/issue-1/moravians-and-john-wesley.html. "If they (the Moravians) were pushed, struck, or thrown down, they rose again and went away; but no complaint was found in their mouth. There was now an opportunity of trying whether they were delivered from the Spirit of fear, as well as from that of pride, anger, and revenge. In the midst of the psalm wherewith their service began, the sea broke over, split the main-sail in pieces, covered the ship, and poured in between the decks, as if the great deep had already swallowed us up. A terrible screaming began among the English. The Germans calmly sung on."

137 Peggy Robins, "God, Man, Woman, and the Wesleys", *Heritage Magazine* 35, no. 3 (1984), https://www.americanheritage.com/god-man-woman-and-wesleys#4. "Oglethorpe had ordered that there be no shooting on Sundays, but the first Sunday he was away from Frederica, Dr. Hawkins, who regarded himself 'above petty regulations,' fired off a gun in the middle of Charles's best sermon. The constable put the doctor in jail for the rest of the day—at the preacher's urging, the constable said later. That afternoon a woman miscarried, which, everyone agreed, would not have happened if the doctor had been available."

138 Ibid, https://www.americanheritage.com/god-man-woman-and-wesleys#3. "He refused Church burial to those who had not received Anglican baptism; and he refused communion to all who had not been baptized by an ordained Episcopal minister."

139 "John Wesley and Women," *Christianity Today*, https://www.christianitytoday.com/ history/issues/issue-2/john-wesley-and-women.html.

140 "John Wesley: Methodical Pietist," *Christianity Today*, https://www.christianitytoday.com/ history/people/denominationalfounders/john-wesley.html.

141 Thomas S. Kidd, *George Whitefield: America's Spiritual Founding Father*, (New Haven, CT: Yale University Press, 2014), 249.

142 Dan Nelson, *A Burning and Shining Light: The Testimony and Witness of George Whitefield* (Somis, CA: LifeSong Publishers, 2017), p. 255, "The origin of evangelical Christianity is traced back to the influence of the awakening movements"; 256, "Many of today's Christians, especially those who think of themselves as 'born again', are his theological heirs" (Cashin, Preface I).

143 Don Stephens (The Renewed Mind), "George Whitefield (1714-1770) - Short biography," September 1, 2019, YouTube, 11:35,https://www.youtube.com/watch?v=ww9lI9pyQ3M, 2:39.

144 Ligonier Ministries, "Steven Lawson: The Evangelistic Zeal of George Whitefield," August 20, 2015, YouTube, 33:37, https://www.youtube.com/watch?v=8ykNKtCv3xk, 2:20.

145 Nelson, *A Burning and Shining Light*, 41.

146 George Whitefield, *The Works of the Reverend George Whitefield* (Edinburgh and London: Dilly, 1771), 18, 19.

147 Nelson, *A Burning and Shining Light*, 31.

148 Arnold A. Dallimore, *George Whitefield: God's Anointed Servant for the Great Revival of the Eighteenth Century* (Wheaton, IL: Crossway, 1990), 29.

149 Ibid, 16.

150 Kidd, *George Whitefield*, 21.

151 Dallimore, *God's Anointed Servant*, 27.

152 Ibid, 26. Because Charles Wesley only lasted seven months in Savannah, Georgia, his brother John invited George Whitefield to leave Oxford and join him in Georgia.

153 Arnold A. Dallimore, *George Whitefield: The Life and Times of the Great Evangelist of the Eighteenth-Century Revival* (Carlisle, PA: Banner of Truth, 1970), p. 114; Dallimore, *God's Anointed Servant*, 29.

154 Kidd, *George Whitefield*, 46.

155 Nelson, *A Burning and Shining Light*, 262, "Both Billy Sunday and Billy Graham followed in Whitefield's footsteps when they made use of tents, athletic stadiums, and other large venues for their meetings."

156 Stephens, "George Whitefield," 7:18.

157 Christian Sermons and Audiobooks, "J. C. Ryle—George Whitefield: His Life and Ministry (Christian audio book)," August 1, 2015, YouTube, 1:34:22,https://www.youtube.com/watch?v=WpHpXLdp4Wk.

158 I'll Be Honest, "The Power of God in George Whitefield's Life—Steve Lawson," March 28, 2010, YouTube, 1:16:24, https://www.youtube.com/watch?v=z4pJgvreFwE, 27:45.

159 Ibid, 28:00.

160 Nelson, *A Burning and Shining Light*, 48.

161 Kidd, *George Whitefield*, 68.; Nelson, p. 65.

162 Southeastern Seminary, "George Whitefield: America's Spiritual Founding Father | Thomas Kidd | PhD," September 13, 2019, YouTube, 34:46, https://www.youtube.com/watch?v=oROKfB3SMqw, 20:22.

163 Peter Hammond, "George Whitefield - Evangelist, Revivalist and Calvinist," Reformation Society of South Africa (blog), March 19, 2014, https://www.reformationsa.org/index.php/history/78-gwhitefield.

164 Ibid.

165 Dallimore, *God's Anointed Servant*, 136.

166 Ibid, 30.

167 Ibid, 36.

168 Ibid, 66.

169 I'll Be Honest, "The Power of God," 54:01.

170 Kidd, *George Whitefield*, 255.

171 Ibid, 1-2.

172 Ibid, 260.

173 Bruce Gore, "37. George Whitefield" https://www.youtube.com/watch?v=hXznIj84DJo (accessed November 30th 2020); Jerome Dean Mahaffey, The Accidental Revolutionary: George Whitefield and the Creation of America (Baylor University Press, Waco, Texas, 2011), "...of all the colonial leaders and their ideas, if you remove Whitefield and his contribution, no one else had the message, popularity, and influence to shape American colonists into people who could declare independence."

174 I'll Be Honest, "The Power of God," 22:16; Southeastern Seminary, "George Whitefield."

175 Elizabeth Whitefield died in 1768 at age 63. "The Life of George Whitefield: a Timeline", http://g.christianbook.com/g/pdf/hp/9781619700611-intro.pdf (Accessed June 14th 2021).

176 George Pears, "The Ultimate Documentary with Insight on George Whitefield," June 6, 2020, YouTube, 37:43 , https://www.youtube.com/watch?v=5zfJ_XnJ7tI, 27:22, 27:53.

177 Dallimore, *God's Anointed Servant*,. 8.

178 Nelson, *A Burning and Shining Light*, 49, 80. The orphanage was Charles Wesley's idea.

179 Dallimore, *God's Anointed Servant*, 77.

180 Pears, "The Ultimate Documentary."

181 Hammond, "George Whitefield.".

182 Kidd, *George Whitefield*, 85.

183 Rick Kennedy, "Did George Whitefield Serve Two Masters?", *Christianity Today*, February 22, 2019, https://www.christianitytoday.com/ct/2019/february-web-only/george-whitefield-peter-choi-evangelist-god-empire.html. "On the campus of the University of Pennsylvania, there sits a statue of one of the school's co-founders: George Whitefield, the 18th-century British evangelist and hero of the Great Awakening. Underneath it, one finds a quote from Benjamin Franklin, the school's other co-founder (and Whitefield's longtime friend): 'I knew him intimately upwards of thirty years. His integrity, disinterestedness and indefatigable zeal in prosecuting every good work I have never seen equaled and shall never see equaled.' "

184 Dallimore, *God's Anointed Servant*, 76.

185 Kidd, *George Whitefield*, 118. Regarding Commissary Garden, Whitefield commented that, "Had an infernal spirit been sent to draw my picture, I think it scarcely possible that he could have painted me in more horrid colours" (Whitefield, Journal, Georgia to Falmouth, 4-7).

186 Dallimore, *God's Anointed Servant*, 83.

187 Kidd, *George Whitefield*, 185.

188 Ibid, 223.

189 Pears, "The Ultimate Documentary," 33:25.

190 *Encyclopedia Britannica*, "Charles Chauncey: American Clergyman [1705-1787]," last updated February 6, 2021, https://www.britannica.com/biography/Charles-Chauncy-American-clergyman-1705-1787; Charles Chauncey, "Seasonable Thoughts on the State of Religion in New-England," Evans Early American Imprint Collection, 1743, https://quod.lib.umich.edu/e/evans/N04182.0001.001/1:6?rgn=div1;view=fulltext. "I shall first mention Itinerant Preaching. This had its Rise (at lest in these Parts) from Mr. WHITEFIELD; though I could never see, I own, upon what Warrant, either from Scripture or Reason, he went about Preaching from one Province and Parish to another, where the Gospel was already preach'd, and by Persons as well qualified for the Work, as he can pretend to be charitably hope, his Design herein was good: But might it not be leavened with some undesirable Mixture? Might he not, at first, take up this Practice from a mistaken Thought of some extraordinary Mission from GOD? Or, from the undue Influence of too high an Opinion of his own Gifts and Graces? And when he had got into this Way, might he not be too much encouraged to go on in it, from the popular Applauses, every where, so liberally heaped on him? If he had not been under too strong a Bias from something or other of this Nature, why so fond of preaching always himself, to the Exclusion, not of his Brethren only, but his Fathers, in Grace and Gifts and Learning, as well as Age? And why so ostentatious and assuming as to alarm so many Towns, by proclaiming his Intentions, in the publick Prints, to preach such a Day in such a Parish, the next Day in such a one, and so on, as he past through the Country; and all this, without the Knowledge, either of Pastors or People in most Places?"

191 Nelson, *A Burning and Shining Light*, 18, 204, "At four years of age, he had a bout with the measles, leaving him with one eye dark blue and causing a squint."

192 Kidd, *George Whitefield*, 18.

193 Ibid, 116.

194 Ibid, 117.

195 Ibid, 115.

196 Ibid, 125.

197 Nelson, *A Burning and Shining Light*, 210.

198 Dallimore, *God's Anointed Servant*, 152.

199 Ibid, 159. Lord Bolingbroke, after hearing Whitefield at Lady Huntington's place, wrote: "[H]is abilities are very considerable—his zeal unquenchable and his piety and excellence genuine."

200 Kidd, *George Whitefield*, 66, 68.

201 Nelson, *A Burning and Shining Light*, 42.

202 I'll Be Honest, "The Power of God," 23:21.

203 Kidd, *George Whitefield*, 263.

204 Dallimore, *God's Anointed Servant*, 15; Nelson, *A Burning and Shining Light*, 46.

205 Kidd, *George Whitefield*, 259.

206 Dallimore, *God's Anointed Servant*, 160.

207 I'll Be Honest, "The Power of God," 19:55.

208 Nelson, *A Burning and Shining Light*, 14.

209 I'll Be Honest, "The Power of God," 31:34.

210 Christian Sermons and Audiobooks, "J. C. Ryle—George Whitefield," 1:24:59.

211 Dallimore, *God's Anointed Servant*, 149.

212 Dick Bohrer (ed), *John Newton: Letters of a Slave Trader Freed by God's Grace* (Chicago: Moody Press, 1982), 24.

213 Ibid, 38: "She said since, that from the first discovery of my regard, and long before the thought was agreeable to her, she had often an unaccountable impression that sooner or later she should be mine."

214 Maryllyn Rouse (ed.), "My Profile (Newton Tells His Own Story)," *The John Newton Project*, January 24, 2014, https://www.johnnewton.org/Groups/222560/The_John_Newton/new_menus/About_John_Newton/About_John_Newton.aspx. "[A]s I was her only child, she made it the chief business and pleasure of her life to instruct me, and bring me up in the nurture and admonition of the Lord. I have been told, that, from my birth, she had, in her mind, devoted me to the ministry; and that, had she lived till I was of a proper age, I was to have been sent to St Andrew's in Scotland to be educated." "When I was four years old, I could read, (hard names excepted,) as well as I can now: and could likewise repeat the answers to the questions in the Assembly's Shorter Catechism, with the proofs; and all Dr. Watt's smaller Catechisms, and his Children's Hymns."

215 "The Love of John and Mary Newton," *Christianity.com*, May 3, 2010, https://www.christianity.com/church/church-history/timeline/1701-1800/the-love-of-john-and-mary-newton-11630257.html.

216 Jonathan Aitken, *John Newton: From Disgrace to Amazing Grace* (Wheaton, IL: Crossway Books, 2007), 29-30.

217 Bohrer, *John Newton*, 85. John Newton's father eventually died in Canada after becoming the Governor of York Fort in Hudson Bay.

218 John Dunn, *A Biography of John Newton* (Adelaide, Australia: New Creation Teaching Ministry, 1994).

219 Bohrer, *John Newton*, 39.

220 David Sheward, "The Real Story Behind 'Amazing Grace'," *Biography.com*, June 15, 2020, https://www.biography.com/news/amazing-grace-story-john-newton.

221 Fellowship Bible Church San Antonio, "Amazing Grace: John Newton," April 16, 2013, YouTube, 6:50, https://www.youtube.com/watch?v=738-231XkkQ; Lindsay Terry, "Story Behind the Song: 'Amazing Grace'," *St. Augustine Record Newspaper*, March 24, 2016, 'https://www.staugustine.com/article/20160324/lifestyle/303249912.

222 Sheward, "The Real Story," "[The song Amazing Grace]…was referenced in Harriet Beecher Stowe's anti-slavery novel *Uncle Tom's Cabin*."

223 Bohrer, *John Newton*, 137: "But the surgeon told her that the malady was too far advanced. The tumor, the size of half a melon, was too large to be removed without danger of her life."

224 "The Love of John and Mary Newton," *Christianity.com*.

225 Ibid.

226 Bohrer, *John Newton*, 118: "Upon Mr. Whitefield's return from America, my two good friends introduced me to him. Although I had little personal acquaintance with him until afterward, his ministry was exceedingly helpful to me."

227 I'll Be Honest, "The Power of God" 5:22.

228 Bohrer, *John Newton*, 112-113: "My first attempt was to learn enough Greek to enable me to understand the New Testament and Septuagint…In the Hebrew, I can read the historical books and psalms with tolerable ease…"

229 Christianity Today: History, "John Newton: Reformed slave trader," *Christianity Today*, 2021, https://www.christianitytoday.com/history/people/pastorsandpreachers/john-newton.html; Oxvision Films, "Amazing Grace: The Story Behind the Song," December 11, 2014, YouTube, 14:29,https://www.youtube.com/watch?v=8m8AHHduTMo. "I usually make a hymn weekly and sometimes it costs me so much thought and study that I hardly do anything else." Sixty-eight of the Olney Hymns were written by William Cowper.

230 Rusty Wright, "Changing Hearts: 'Amazing Grace' Hymn Writer's Racist Past," *CBN.com*, 2020, https://www1.cbn.com/music/changing-hearts-amazing-grace-hymn-writers-racist-past.

231 Wright, "Changing Hearts."

232 While dying, John Newton said "I am a great sinner and Christ is a great saviour." https://www.goodreads.com/quotes/26320-although-my-memory-s-fading-i-remember-two-things-very-clearly (accessed June 14th 2021).

233 Mary Drewery, *William Carey: A Biography* (Grand Rapids, MI: Zondervan Publishing House, 1978), 16.

234 Ibid, 102, "The conscientious but unsuccessful shoemaker, the penniless pastor, the frustrated idealist of Northampshire are replaced by a dedicated man of maturity and poise;"; Ibid, 7, "[A]n obscure village Paulerspury."

235 Ibid, 11, quoting Carey: "I chose to read books of science, history, voyages, more than any others." Ibid, 30. Carey was (fascinated) reading The Last Voyage of Captain Cook. "No one would ever venture to introduce Christianity to them because neither fame nor profit would offer the prerequisite inducement" the book gave him a Macedonian call."

236 Ibid, 12, "He was nicknamed Columbus by the village boys."

237 Ibid 12, " I was addicted to swearing, lying, and unchaste conversation"; Ibid 13, "Carey tells us that 'he sometimes drank rather too freely' (abused alcohol) and 'was an inveterate enemy to lying, a vice to which I was awfully addicted'."

238 Ibid, 12.

239 Ibid, 13, "He suffered from a skin disease that made it painful for him to go out in the full sun. If his face and hands were exposed to the sun for any lengthy period, he would suffer agony throughout the night."

240 Galen B. Royer, "William Carey: The Father of Modern Missions," *Wholesome Words*, 2021, https://www.wholesomewords.org/missions/bcarey3.html.

241 Bruce Gore, "40. Carey," March 25, 2015, YouTube, 48:05, https://www.youtube.com/watch?v=d5KNYyvx4d8.

242 Kellsye M. Finnie, *William Carey: By Trade a Cobbler* (Bromley, UK: STL Books, 1986), 32.

243 Finnie, 42.

244 H. Miriam Ross, "What About Dorothy?", *Missio Nexus*, October 1, 1992, https://missionexus.org/what-about-dorothy/.

245 Ruth A. Tucker, "William Carey's Less-than-Perfect Family Life," *Christian History Institute*, 1992, https://christianhistoryinstitute.org/magazine/article/william-careys-less-than-perfect-family-life.

246 Drewery, *William Carey*, 163, "William Wilberforce commented in 1813: 'Now the Slave Trade is abolished, the exclusion of missionaries from India is by far the greatest of our national sins.' He presented 837 petitions to Parliament representing over half a million signatures. He enlisted the aid of the churches, of the missionary societies, and of the Abolitionists who had supported his campaign against slavery."

247 Ibid, 163.

248 Ibid, 164. Wilberforce called them "these good and great men." Drewery, p. 164 "The first person to receive a license from the Company to work openly in India as a missionary was Carey's nephew, Eustace."

249 Ibid, 127, "Carey produced six grammars of Bengali, Sanskrit, Marathi, Panjabi, Telugi, and Kanarese, and with John Clark Marshman, one of Bhutia."; Drewery, p. 155 "Carey's polyglot dictionary giving the equivalent of each Sanskrit word in every language of Asia, would have been a work of supreme philological importance (destroyed in the 1812 fire)."

250 Ibid, 156, Carey "translated the whole Bible into Bengali, Oriya, Marathi, Hindi, Assamese, and Sanskrit, and parts of it into twenty-nine other languages or dialects"; Ibid, 156, "It is this breadth of vision of making God's Word available to all humanity in its own tongue that is Carey's chief glory."

251 Ibid, 151, 159, "[T]he Serampore missionaries contributed to the renaissance of Indian Literature in the nineteenth century."

252 Ibid, 220. "In 1818 Carey founded two magazines and a newspaper, the Samachar Darpan, the first newspaper printed in any Asian language."

253 Ruth Mangalwadi and Vishal Mangalwadi, *William Carey: A Tribute by an Indian Woman* (New Delhi, India: Nindivet Good Books, 1993), 6, "[H]e was the father of printing technology. Built what was then the largest printing press in India."

254 Ibid, 8, Carey "pioneered the idea of lending libraries in India."; Ibid, 6. Carey "introduced the steam engine to India."

255 Ibid, 6, "Carey introduced the steam engine to India and was the first to make indigenous paper for the publishing industry. He introduced the concept of a 'Savings Bank' to India, in order to fight the all-pervasive social evil of usury at interest rates of 36% to 72%."

256 Ibid, 7. Carey "was the founder of the Agri-Horticultural Society in the 1820s, thirty years before the Royal Agricultural Society was established in England."

257 Ibid, 8, Carey "was the first person in India to write about forest conservation."

258 Drewery, *William Carey*, 186, Carey "was elected in 1823 as a Fellow of the Linnean Society of London, one of the world's most distinguished botanical societies. His favorite flowers were lilies…he had the honour of having one (Careyanum) named after him…"

259 Mangalwadi and Mangalwadi, William Carey, 9, Carey "was the first man to stand out against the oppression of women through Sati widow burning and female infanticide."

260 Bruce Gore, "40. Carey," 48:00; Asha Basumatary, "Study of Institution of Female Infanticide in Colonial India," *Journal of International Academic Research for Multidisciplinary* 3, no. 7 (2015): 404, http://www.jiarm.com/AUG2015/paper24262.pdf.

261 Drewery, *William Carey*, 220. Carey "protested widow-burning; it was banned in 1829."

262 Mangalwadi and Mangalwadi, 6, Carey "campaigned for humane treatment of lepers who were being burned or buried alive because of their bad karma. The fifth phase of bad karma was leprosy."

263 David Livingstone, *Missionary Travels* (London: Ward, Lock and Co Limited, 1913), 14.

264 Ibid, 6, "[T]he opium war was then raging, and it was deemed inexpedient for me to proceed to China. I had fondly hoped to have gained access to that then closed empire by means of the healing arts."

265 Ibid 434, 460, "Walking down to the forest, after telling these poor people for the first time in their lives, that the Son of God had so loved us as to come down from heaven to save them."

266 Ibid, 474.

267 Ibid, 15.

268 Ibid, 161, "I explained to him (Chief Sekelutu) that my object was to elevate him and his people to be Christians; but he replied that he did not wish to learn to read the Book, for he was afraid 'it might change his heart, and make him content with only one wife, like Sechele.'"

269 Ed Hird and Janice Hird, "Revolutionary Love in East Africa," *EdHird's Blog*, May 17, 2018, https://edhird.com/2018/05/17/revolutionary-love/.

270 "David Livingstone Quotes," *Goodreads*, 2021, https://www.goodreads.com/author/quotes/211925.David_Livingstone.

271 Ibid, 15, 66, "Back in England, which he hadn't seen since leaving in 1840, Livingstone became a national hero. He was an adventurous cipher, a man few knew personally, but who was single-handedly charting the African interior in the name of God and country."

272 Ibid, 15.

273 Ibid, 6, "The effect of travel on a man whose heart is in the right place is that the mind is made more self-reliant: It becomes more confident of its own resources — there is greater presence of mind."

274 Cynthia O'Brien, *Travel with the Great Explorers* (St. Catherine's, ON: Crabtree Publishing Company, 2017), 4, "If you have men who will only come if there is a good road, I don't want them. I want men who will come if there is no road at all."

275 Livingstone, *Missionary Travels*, 7. Writing, for Livingstone the best-selling author, was agony: "I think I would rather cross the African continent again than undertake to write another book. It is far easier to travel than to write about it."

276 Dugard, *Into Africa*, 67, "The recent repeal of a stamp tax made newspapers affordable to the masses for the first time. Britain's population of four million was one of the world's most literate and were becoming zealots for news…Crowds mobbed him on the streets and even in church. He was given the keys to cities…"

277 Cooke, *Exploration*, 15.

278 Livingstone, *Missionary Travels*, 579.

279 Dugard, *Into Africa*, 2, "He had walked across the Kalahari Desert, traced the path of the Zambezi River, and ambled from one side of Africa to the other."

280 Livingstone, *Missionary Travels*, 445

281 Ibid, 404.

282 John Telford, "Mary Livingstone," *Wholesome Words*, 2021, https://www.wholesomewords.org/missions/blivingmary1.html.

283 Telford, "Mary Livingstone."

284 Dugard, *Into Africa*, 2. The London newspapers reported his death on several occasions.

285 Ibid, 308, "American journalists of the era even voted Stanley's discovery of Livingstone 'the story of the century'."

286 Ibid, 284; Stanley said of Livingstone, "In him, religion exhibits its loveliest of features. It governs his conduct towards all that come in contact with him."

287 Ibid, 288.

288 Ibid, 278.

289 Ibid, 290. The Queen through Lord Granville thanked Stanley. "Her Majesty's high appreciation of the prudence and zeal…relieving her Majesty from the anxiety which, in common with her subjects, she had felt in regard of that distinguished traveler."

290 Ibid, 66. Portugal, which was heavily involved in the Slave trade, pressured England into recalling Livingstone as British Consul.

291 Ibid, 66.

292 Ibid, 67, "Livingstone resigned from the London Missionary Society to focus his work exclusively on ending the slave trade through his 'three C's' -Christianity, commerce, and cotton (later amended to 'colonialism'). He felt that an influx of legitimate trade to the interior would empower the natives. His new employer was the British Foreign Office, which officially designated him Consul to the Tribes of Africa."

293 Livingstone, *Missionary Travels*, 60.

294 Dugard, *Into Africa*, 63.

295 Tim Cooke, *The Exploration of Africa*, (New York: Garth Stevens Publishing, 2013), 38, "The most famous of all African explorers."

296 Martin Dugard, *Into Africa: The Epic Adventures of Stanley and Livingstone*, (New York: Broadway Books, 2003), 15, "In an era when no occupation was more glamorous than African explorer."

297 Bruce Gore, "41. Livingstone," March 24, 2015, YouTube, 54:26, https://www.youtube.com/watch?v=b_8UlNn5UrQ, 34:00.

298 Westminster Abbey, "David Livingstone: Writer, Explorer, Physician, and Doctor," https://www.westminster-abbey.org/abbey-commemorations/commemorations/david-livingstone, "Livingstone's heart had been buried under a mpundu tree but his faithful attendants enclosed his embalmed body in a cylinder of bark which was wrapped in sailcloth and carried it to the coast and then sailed to London, arriving the following year. As the Doctor had been away from England for so long a correct identification of the remains was required and this was verified by the badly set broken arm which had been crushed by a lion."

299 Gore, "41. Livingstone," 50:10.

300 Robert Sandall, *The History of the Salvation Army, 1878-1886, vol. 2* (London: Thomas Nelson and Sons, 1950), 343, "*The Pall Mall Gazette, May* 29th 1886 'the supreme distinction of the Salvation Army is that it has done more to realize the ideals of almost every social reformer, secular or religious, than any other organization we can name'."

301 Charles Dickens, *Letters of Charles Dickens: 1833-1870*, eds. Georgina Hogarth and Mary Dickens, (Cambridge: Cambridge University Press, 2011), 451.

302 Peter Ackroyd, *Thames: Sacred River* (London: Vintage, 2008).

303 Leslie Ludy, "Catherine Booth: Relentless Spiritual Passion," *Revive Our Hearts* (blog), April 28, 2016, https://www.reviveourhearts.com/true-woman/blog/catherine-booth-life-relentless-spiritual-passion/.

304 Maxwell Ryan, "The Gospel of Vegetarianism," *Salvationist* (blog), October 5, 2010, https://salvationist.ca/articles/2010/10/the-gospel-of-vegetarianism/. "Early in their marriage she wrote to William, 'Have you thought any more about vegetarianism? I am inclined towards it more than ever. I am convinced of the importance of simplicity and regularity in diet...I don't think half as highly of meat (animal food I mean) as I used to do'."

305 "Booth, Catherine (1829–1890)," *Encyclopedia.com, 2021* , https://www.encyclopedia.com/women/encyclopedias-almanacs-transcripts-and-maps/booth-catherine-1829-1890, "[O]n one occasion she almost lost her life by jumping out of a moving carriage in order to prevent a boy from causing further injury to a donkey he was hitting with a heavy-headed hammer."

306 "Catherine Booth," *New World Encyclopedia*, 2021, https://www.newworldencyclopedia.org/entry/Catherine_Booth.

307 Robert Sandall, *The History of the Salvation Army, 1865-1878, vol. 1,* (London: Thomas Nelson and Sons, 1947), 16, "The Primitive Methodists (Sheffield, June 1862) did not waste words, but bluntly declared, 'That Conference urges all station authorities to avoid the employing of revivalists so-called.' "

308 Norman H. Murdoch, "Army Mother," *Christian History*, 26 (1990), https://www.christianitytoday.com/history/issues/issue-26/army-mother.html.

309 Lauren Martin, "Some of My Best Men Are Women," *Others Magazine, Australia*, https://others.org.au/army-archives/some-of-my-best-men-are-women/ .

310 Christine Parkin, "Pioneer in Female Ministry," *Christian History Institute* (1990), https://christianhistoryinstitute.org/magazine/article/pioneer-in-female-ministry.

311 Kelly Craft, "Ambassador Craft's Remarks to the Salvation Army National Advisory Board Dinner," *US Embassy in Canada News* (blog), September 27, 2018, https://ca.usembassy.gov/ambassador-crafts-remarks-to-the-salvation-army-national-advisory-board-dinner/. "Your founding mother, on the other hand, Catherine Booth will be forever remembered for her work directly lobbying Queen Victoria to pass Parliamentary legislation for the protection of girls to safeguard them from child prostitution. The year was

1884 and the Salvation Army collected 340,000 signatures to Parliament to help ensure the bill received passage and Royal Assent."

312 John Simkin, "Catherine Booth," *Spartacus Educational,* 1997, https://spartacus-educational.com/Wbooth.htm.

313 Sandall, *The History of the Salvation Army* 2, 221.

314 Salvation Army Australia, "Founders William and Catherine Booth," 2021, https://www.salvationarmy.org.au/about-us/our-story/our-history/founders-william-and-catherine-booth/.

315 Robert Sandall, *The History of the Salvation Army, 1883-1953,* Volume 3 (London: Thomas Nelson and Sons, 1955), 64.

316 "How William and Catherine Booth started The Salvation Army," *New Frontier Chronicle,* July 2, 2019, https://www.newfrontierchronicle.org/how-william-and-catherine-booth-started-the-salvation-army/.

317 John Branston, "Christian Soldiers: The Salvation Army brings humility and $48 million to the fairgrounds discussion," *Memphis Flyer,* November 18, 2005.

318 Sandall, *The History of the Salvation Army* 2, 183.

319 Ibid, 181.

320 Ibid, 181. Bonnett: "[C]heap, strong and large enough to protect the head of wearers from cold as well as from brickbats and other missiles"; 174, Basingstoke, in 1880, described, "[H]eavy sticks crashing upon our soldiers' heads, laying them open, saturating them in blood, other with cut faces."

321 "Catherine Booth: Breast Cancer Awareness," *Salvation Army Ministry to Women* (blog), http://www.sawomensministries.org/blog/breastcancerawareness/.

322 Sue Young, "Catherine Booth 1829 - 1890 and William Booth 1829—1912,", *Sue Young Histories* (blog), December 7, 2007, https://www.sueyounghistories.com/2007-12-07-catherine-booth-and-homeopathy/; Sandal, *The History of the Salvation Army* 3, 134.

323 Womens Ministries USA South, "William's Eulogy for Catherine," October 4, 2016, YouTube, 6:01, https://youtu.be/Chkhn9-t3MQ.

324 "Catherine Booth Quotes," *AllGreatQuotes* (blog), https://www.allgreatquotes.com/quote-88470/.

325 A.E. Thompson, *A.B. Simpson: His Life and Work* (Chicago, IL: Moody Publishers, 2009), 46.

326 "Take the Full Gospel to the World," Healing and Revival Press, 2004, https://www.healingandrevival.com/BioABSimpson.htm.

327 A.B. Simpson, "Himself," *Bible Believers,* 2021, https://www.biblebelievers.com/simpson-ab_himself.html. "Once it was the blessing, Now it is the Lord; Once it was the feeling, Now it is His Word. Once His gifts I wanted, Now the Giver own; Once I sought for healing, Now Himself alone."

328 John G. Lake, *John G. Lake: The Complete Collection of his Life Teachings,* ed. Roberts Liardon (Tulsa, OK: Albury Publishing, 1999), 9.

329 John G. Lake and Kenneth Copeland, *John G. Lake: His Life, His Sermons, His Boldness of Faith* (Fort Worth, TX: Kenneth Copeland Publications, 1994), xiii.

330 Ibid, xvi.

331 Ibid, xx.

332 Ibid, 484.

333 Ibid, 749.

334 Ibid, xxiv.

335 Ibid 207.

336 Ibid, 236.

337 Ibid, 3.

338 Ibid, xxvii; Lake, *The Complete Collection,* 78.

339 Lake, *The Complete Collection,* xxvi.

340 Lake and Copeland, *His Life,* xxvii.

341 Ibid, xviii

342 Ibid, 422

343 Ibid, 173

344 Ibid, 163, "Through this healing ministry, the Church at Spokane reports 100,000 heal-ings by the power of God through five years of continuous daily efforts"; Lake, *The Complete Collection*, 688.

345 Lake, *The Complete Collection*, 9.

346 Lake and Copeland, *His Life*, 258.

347 Ibid, xxi

348 Lake, *The Complete Collection*, 688, "Having previously been a manager for a life insur-ance company, his extensive business experience caused many business people to be more open to the gospel."

349 Lake and Copeland, *His Life*, xxiv

350 Ibid, 255, 286, "When they used the Name [of Jesus], power struck. The dynamite of heaven exploded."

351 Vision Video, "A Diary of Revival—The Outbreak of the 1904 Welsh Awakening," May 24, 2017, Vimeo, 1:02:00, https://vimeo.com/ondemand/adiaryofrevival.

352 Brynmor Pierce Jones, *An Instrument of Revival: The Complete Life of Evan Roberts, 1878-1951* (Newberry, FL: Bridge-Logos Foundation, 1995), 15; Roberts Liardon, *God's Generals* (New Kensington, PA: Whitaker House, 1996), 82.

353 Watchmanforwales, "1 of 2: Evan Roberts & The 1904/05 Welsh Revival," May 14, 2021, YouTube, 6:11,

https://www.youtube.com/watch?v=ACGbasEBjmM.

354 Ibid.

355 James Stewart, *Invasion of Wales by the Spirit through Evan Roberts* (Fort Washington, PA: Christian Literature Crusade, 1963), 28. To his future brother-in-law Sydney Evans, Evan Roberts said, "I've had a vision all Wales being lifted up to heaven. We are going to see the greatest revival that Wales has ever had known — and the Holy Spirit is coming now…Do you believe that God can give us 100,000 souls now?"

356 David Matthews, *I Saw the Welsh Revival* (Chicago, IL: Moody Press, 1957), 41.

357 Ibid, 19.

358 Stewart, *Invasion*, 68.

359 Matthews, *I Saw the Welsh Revival*, 83, "Guidance and obedience were the words crossing his lips with almost monotonous reiteration…Mr Roberts urged abandonment to the will of God."

360 Ibid, 92.

361 Ibid, 82, "Wherever he (Evan) felt the liberty of the Spirit in a service, his eyes glistened, his face became almost transformed, and his smile radiant."; South Wales Daily News, 18 Nov 1904, 'His (Evan's) smile lights up his face. He has a pleasant face, rather boyish, perhaps, long and thin and clean shaven, and topped with wavy brown hair.'

362 Ibid, 95, Evan Roberts said in *The Western Mail* newspaper: "You desire an outpouring of the Holy Spirit in your city? You do well. But remember, four conditions must be observed. They are essential. First, is there any sin in your past in which you have not honestly dealt, —not confessed to God? On your knees at once. Your past must be put away and cleansed… Second… Have you forgiven everybody—Everybody? If not, don't expect forgiveness for your sins… Third, do what the Holy Spirit prompts without hesitation or fear. Obedience—prompt, implicit, unquestioning obedience, at whatever cost. Fourth, a public confession of Christ as public Saviour… Hear the words of the Lord: 'Quench not the Holy Spirit'. That is the only way to Revival. When the fire burns, it purifies. And when purified, you are fit to be used in the work of the Lord."

363 Ibid, 24, "At every service, Evan emphasized the words "Obey the Holy Spirit… Be filled with the Holy Spirit."

364 Stewart, *Invasion*, 13, "[H]e became by far the most publicized preacher in the world."

365 R. P. Pope and R. Pope, "Demythologizing the Evan Roberts Revival," *Journal of Ecclesiastical History* 57, no. 3 (2006):515-534; Awstin, *The Religious Revival in Wales* (Bishop's Waltham, UK: Revival Library, 1905), i, ii, 10, 31.

366 Liardon, *God's Generals*, 87

367 Kevin Adams and Emyr Jones, *A Pictorial History of Revival: The Outbreak of the 1904 Welsh Awakening* (Surrey, UK: CWR, 2004), 91, "Lloyd George the MP for Caernarvon District showed a great interest in the revival even cancelling political meetings so that they would not clash."

368 Pope and Pope, "Demythologizing," 515-534; R. Tudor Jones, *Ffydd ac argyfwng cenedl: Hanes crefydd yng Nghymru 1890–1914* (Swansea, UK: Dryswch a diwygiad, 1982), 214.; Stewart, *Invasion*, 9, "While the Spirit's workings in revival spread to almost every nook and corner of the country, the ministry of Evan Roberts was in the main confined to one of the twelve counties. The fire of God burned in towns and villages where he did not visit. And in many places where he did visit, he found the fire was already there. His visit only fanned the flame."

369 Watchmanforwales, "1 of 2: Evan Roberts.")

370 Matthews, *I Saw the Welsh Revival*, 71.

371 Watchmanforwales, "1 of 2: Evan Roberts."

372 Pope and Pope, "Demythologizing," 515-534; Evan Roberts, "Cenadwri at eglwys Dduw," *Y Traethodydd lx* (1905), 320.

373 Awstin, *Religious Revival*, i, 2.; Pope and Pope, "Demythologizing," 515-534.

374 Matthews, *I Saw the Welsh Revival*, 80. One man, with his rejoicing, weeping wife by his side, thanked God that Jesus had turned beer into furniture in his home; Pope and Pope, "Demythologizing," 515-534, "Glamorgan saw a drop in drunkenness convictions from 10,000 in 1903 to 5,490 in 1906."

375 Servantandfriend, "God's Generals—Evan Roberts," October 21, 2013, YouTube, 1:06:34, https://www.youtube.com/watch?v=6Jqmju1CaOo.

376 King's Way Church, " 'The Welsh Revival & Azusa Street Revival' God's Generals Session 4 with Roberts Liardon," October 14, 2016, YouTube, 2:48:08, https://www.youtube.com/watch?v=TdszszDp9lk.

377 Servantandfriend, "God's Generals."

378 Watchmanforwales, "1 of 2: Evan Roberts."

379 Ibid.

380 Pope and Pope, "Demythologizing," 515-534; Sidney Evans and Gomer M. Roberts, *Cyfrol goffa diwygiad, 1904-1905* (Caernarfon, UK: Methodistiaid Calfinaidd, 1954), 73.

381 Matthews, *I Saw the Welsh Revival*, 42.

382 Pope and Pope, "Demythologizing," 525-534, "The revival meetings…were often led by young people and were known for spontaneity and a breaking down of old barriers of formality. Much was made of prayer and open confession"; Liardon, *God's Generals*, 86.

383 Matthews, *I Saw the Welsh Revival*, 43.

384 Servantandfriend, "God's Generals"; Liardon, *God's Generals*, 85 "Some (revival) meetings lasted until 4am with crowds gathering outside for 6am prayer."; Stewart, *Invasion*, 17

385 Matthews, *I Saw the Welsh Revival*, 44.

386 Pope and Pope, "Demythologizing," 515-534, "Beyond Britain, revival also broke out in countries to which the Welsh had been sent as missionaries, such as in India among the Khasia Hills and in Madagascar, among Welsh expatriates in the United States, and in South America…in France…in Norway, Denmark, Holland, Silesia, Hungary, Latvua, Bulgaria, Russia, Algiers, South Africa, Australia, and New Zealand"; Awstin, *Religious Revival*, iii, 13-14, Evan Roberts commented,"The Spirit which prevailed so largely in Wales today would spread not only to England but throughout the world."

387 Watchmanforwales, "1 of 2: Evan Roberts."

388 Ibid; Adams and Jones, *A Pictorial History*, 64, "After the Blaenanerch experience on Sept 29th 1904, Evan wrote to a friend: 'I've received three great blessings: 1) I have lost all nervousness. 2) I can sing all day. 3) What an easy thing it is to give thanks now."

389 Stewart, *Invasion*, 15.

390 Watchmanforwales, "1 of 2: Evan Roberts."

391 Ibid; Adams and Jones, *A Pictorial History*, 95, "Evan Roberts' favorite Welsh revival hymn was Great God of Wonders."

392 Pope and Pope, "Demythologizing," 515-534; Awstin, "Religious Revial," 6.

393 Servantandfriend, "God's Generals"; Liardon, *God's Generals*, 88, "Evan Roberts only slept two or three hours a night (during the first two months of the revival),"; 89, "Whenever friends would encourage him to rest, he reacted strongly against it."

394 King's Way Church, "Welsh Revival." Exhaustion kills revivals. We, like Evans, need to learn to pace ourselves.

395 Matthews, *I Saw the Welsh Revival*, 116, "Every attempt to see him was frustrated… He refused to see his father and brother"; Servantandfriend, "God's Generals."

396 Mahatma Gandhi, *An Autobiography: The Story of My Experiments with Truth* (General Press, New Delhi, India, 1958), 49.

397 E. Stanley Jones, *A Song of Ascents: A Spiritual Autobiography* (Nashville, TN: Abingdon, 1968), 133-134.

398 Tom Albin, "The Spiritual Vision and Mission of E. Stanley Jones," (Paper presented at The Thirteenth Oxford Institute of Methodist Theological Studies, Christ Church, New Zealand, 12–19 August 2013), https://oimts.files.wordpress.com/2013/09/2013-4-albin.pdf, 1, "By the end of his life, he had published twenty-eight books, two of which sold over one million copies.")

399 Albin, "Spiritual Vision," 1, "It is widely agreed that E. Stanley Jones was one of the greatest Methodist missionaries to India, North America, and indeed to the world."; "E. Stanley Jones: Missionary and Founder of United Christian *Ashrams*," *United Christian Ashrams, 2020*, http://www.christianashram.org/e-stanley-jones.html; Richard W. Taylor, "The Legacy of E. Stanley Jones,"
International Bulletin, July 1982, http://www.internationalbulletin.org/issues/1982-03/1982-03-102-taylor.pdf.

400 Albin, "Spiritual Vision," 1, "In their 1964 *Times* edition, they stated that Jones' only peer in international Christian ministry was the Rev. Billy Graham"; Stephen Neill, *Salvation Tomorrow* (Nashville: Abingdon, 1976), 26, "in his great days Jones was probably (second to C.F. Andrews alone) the best-known western Christian in the whole of India."

401 Thomas John Philip Nalloor, "Dr. E. Stanley Jones (3 Jan 1884-25 Jan 1973)," The Mar Thoma Parish, Dubai, E-Library, 2012, https://www.dubaimarthomaparish.org/links/e-lib/E.Stanley%20Jones.pdf; Samuel Matthew, "E. Stanley Jones and His Interfaith Exercise," FULLER Studio, 2021, https://fullerstudio.fuller.edu/e-stanley-jones-and-his-interfaith-exercise/, "He (Jones) was a highly skilled orator, known to easily draw an audience of four to five hundred educated Hindus and Muslims in any city that he visited."

402 David R. Swartz, "Christ of the American Road: E. Stanley Jones, India, and Civil Rights," *Journal of American Studies*, 51 (October 10, 2017), https://www.cambridge.org/core/journals/journal-of-american-studies/article/abs/christ-of-the-american-road-e-stanley-jones-india-and-civil-rights/7ED2EA879A189165344DAD4AD9576B3B: 1132, an undated, unattributed biographical sketch of Jones, Box 1, Folder 3; Box 5, Folders 5 and 6, ATSSC; E. Stanley Jones, "Higher Synthesis?" *The Christian Century*, August 14, 1957, 970, "After talking personally with Billy Graham, I became convinced that he is more or less consciously one of the meeting places of this movement toward synthesis. And therefore this movement is to be welcomed. It is a movement of the Spirit."

403 Billy Graham, *Nearing Home* (Nashville, TN: Thomas Nelson, 2011), 33.

404 Albin, "Spiritual Vision," 2; Tom Albin, "Brother E. Stanley Jones," *Good News* (blog), May 16, 2019, https://goodnewsmag.org/2019/05/brother-e-stanley-jones/, "Jones suffered a ruptured appendix that proved to be inoperable. The pain of his illness was compounded to the expanding responsibilities; Stanley was assigned one district with more than one million people, then another and another until he was responsible for four

districts and the Methodist Publishing House in Lucknow. The stress and the physical ill-ness was too much: 'As a consequence, at the end of eight and a half years I was ordered to go to America on furlough…. I was at the back of the church kneeling in prayer, not for myself but for others, when God said to me: 'Are you yourself ready for the work to which I have called you?' My reply: 'No, Lord, I'm done for. I've reached the end of my resources and I can't go on.' 'If you'll turn that problem over to me and not worry about it, I'll take care of it.' My eager reply: 'Lord, I close the bargain right here.' I arose from my knees knowing I was a well man."

405 Albin, "Brother E. Stanley Jones,", "That exchange is marked by a plaque on the Lucknow church wall, it reads: 'Near this spot Stanley Jones knelt a physically broken man and arose a physically well man'."

406 E. Stanley Jones, *Mahatma Gandhi: An Interpretation* (Lucknow: Lucknow Publishing House, 1948; reprinted 1963), 36.; E. Stanley Jones, "My Stay at Santineketan," *Indian Witness*, September 5, 1923, 612f; *Jones circular letter*, October 1, 1926, Box 10, Folder 6, ATSSC, in Swartz, "Christ of the American Road," After meeting Gandhi at the Sabarmati Ashram, Jones commented to his American supporters, "The spirit of the ashram is so beautiful and so self-sacrificial, Gandhi combines strength and humility, unselfishness and service."

407 Swartz, "Christ of the American Road," 1124, There was at the Sat Tal Ashram in India "…a large painting of Christ with an inscription that read, "Christ is the Guru of this Ashram.")

408 William E. Berg, "My Spiritual Journey with Brother Stanley," in "600 Faculty/Staff: E. Stanley Jones Biographical," AU Archives, in Swartz, "Christ of the American Road."

409 Many members of our family have been powerfully impacted by the almost fifty years of the BC Christian Ashram www.bcchristianashram.com .

410 Kathryn Reese Hendershot, "E. Stanley Jones Had a Wife: The Life and Missiological Contributions of Dr. Mabel Lossing Jones, Missionary to India, 1878-1978," Ph.D. diss. (Asbury Theological Seminary, 2005), https://place.asburyseminary.edu/ecommonsatsdissertations/16/. Being a remarkable leader herself, Mabel Slossing Jones sat on the Municipal Council of Sitapur with ten Hindu men and ten Muslim men for 20 years (the only woman, the only Christian, the only non-Indian).

411 Jones, *A Song of Ascent*, 83.

412 Hendershot, "E. Stanley Jones Had a Wife," 279.

413 Albin, "Spiritual Vision," 6-7, "Jones describes the first round table conference as an accidental creation. After a public lecture and question and answer session sometime in 1923, a Hindu chairperson of a public lecture asked if they could schedule a more private session with a small group of the city's "leading figures." The chairperson suggested a tea party for a smaller group of people, which would allow for a more personal conversation than even a question and answer session afforded. Jones agreed and by 1925 these smaller gatherings became integral to his ministry and a regular part of his public lectureships."

414 Ibid, 7, Matthews states, "Their discussions revolved around what religion brought in terms of light, of inward peace and harmony, of redemption from sin and from the power of this world, of God and what they are verifying as true in experience."

415 Matt Kinnell, "E. Stanley Jones," Asbury College Archives, https://www.asbury.edu/academics/resources/library/archives/biographies/e-stanley-jones/.

416 *The Christian Century* 81 (Feb. 12, 1964), 216.; Albin, "Spiritual Vision," 1, "In 1962, [Jones] was nominated for the Nobel Peace Prize and in 1963 Dr. Jones received the Gandhi Peace Prize."

417 Swartz, "Christ of the American Road," in an NBC radio broadcast, Feb. 17th of an unknown year, Box 33, Folder 21, ATSSC. 'For India.'.

418 Ibid," 1125.

419 Albin, "Spiritual Vision," 1, "His work as a liaison between Roosevelt and Japanese diplo-mats in October and November of 1941 is seen by some as almost avoiding (if only post-poning) the Japanese attack on Pearl Harbor."

420 Swartz, "Christ of the American Road, 1126.

421 Ibid, 1134, Jones to Jesse Arnup, Jan. 20th 1944, Box 4, Folder 1, ATSSC.

422 Ibid, James Farmer to John F. Kennedy, April 26th 1961, in Martin Luther King Jr. Papers Project.

423 Howard A. Snyder, "Profiles: E. Stanley Jones: Mission / Evangelism," *Catalyst*, March 1, 2010, https://www.catalystresources.org/e-stanley-jones/.

424 Albin, "Spiritual Vision," 2, "His visits to Russia and his public reflections on communism brought unwanted attention from the FBI."

425 Swartz, "Christ of the American Road, 1121, "In front of an audience of thirty thousand people on the southern tip of the subcontinent, Jones desperately sought to sway Indians away from Communism. In the midst of many Communist leaders and a tense atmosphere, Jones reported success. Many 'found Christ as their personal Savior'."

426 Ibid, 1128.

427 Daniel Mark Epstein, *Sister Aimee: the Life of Aimee Semple McPherson* (San Diego, CA: Harcourt Brace & Company, 1993), 156, 260, "the most famous woman in America"; Gary Krist, "Op-Ed: Aimee Semple McPherson: The L. A. Evangelist Who Built the World's First Megachurch," *LA Times*, June 24,2018, https://www.latimes.com/opinion/op-ed/la-oe-krist-aimee-semple-mcpherson-20180624-story.html, "Given how famous she was in her day, it's remarkable how little McPherson is remembered today, even in the place she called home."

428 A personal text, following a phone call, from Pastor Barry Buzza of Northside Church in Coquitlam, BC, October 9, 2019.

429 "Aimee Semple McPherson: AMERICAN RELIGIOUS LEADER," *Encyclopedia Britannica*, 2020, https://www.britannica.com/biography/Aimee-Semple-McPherson.

430 Epstein, *Sister Aimee*, 52.

431 Aimee Semple McPherson and Raymond L. Cox, *Aimee: Life Story of Aimee Semple McPherson* (Los Angeles, CA: Foursquare Publications, 1979), 25.

432 Chris Hollowaty, "Sister Aimee, St Patrick and the Triune God: Where are We From, Where are We Going?" M.A. thesis, (Seattle School of Theology and Psychology, 2015), https://www.academia.edu/12934888/Sister_Aimee_St_Patrick_and_the_Triune_God_Where_Are_We_From_Where_Are_We_Going.

433 Christian History Magazine Editorial Staff, "Aimee Semple McPherson: Foursquare phenomenon," *Christianity Today Online*, 2019, https://www.christianitytoday.com/history/people/denominationalfounders/aimee-semple-mcpherson.html.

434 McPherson and Cox, *Aimee*, 80, Aimee said: "Everyone goes to a fire. Let's go out and ring the alarm." Using her gift for drama, she stood on a chair like a statue in the middle of town until a crowd gathered.

435 Douglas H. Rudd, *Aimee Semple McPherson: Canadian-born Evangelist* (Belleville, ON: Guardian Books, 2006), 79.

436 Epstein, *Sister Aimee*, 208. Aimee later commented in San Diego, "As soon as one was healed, she ran and told nine others, and brought them too, even telegraphing and rushing the sick in on trains."

437 Rudd, *Aimee Semple McPherson*, 97.

438 Peter Carlson, "American Schemers: Aimee Semple McPherson," HistoryNet, August 2018, https://www.historynet.com/american-schemers-aimee-semple-mcpherson.htm.

439 Krist, "Aimee Semple McPherson.".

440 Naomi Grimley, Naomi, "The mysterious disappearance of a celebrity preacher," BBC News, November 25, 2014, https://www.bbc.com/news/magazine-30148022. BBC News

441 Rudd, *Aimee Semple McPherson*, 97.

442 "From the Archives: Aimee Semple McPherson Dies Suddenly in Oakland," *LA Times*, September 28, 1944, https://www.latimes.com/local/obituaries/archives/la-me-aimee-semple-mcpherson-19440928-story.html.

443 Epstein, *Sister Aimee*, 390.

444 Private text response from Laura Lynn Tyler Thompson, January 10, 2019.

445 Rudd, *Aimee Semple McPherson*, 103, "She ignored numerous notes threatening kidnapping or death. On one occasion, a man who had been writing hostile notes with threats to blow up the Temple, forced his way into her home." Early in 1925, the police uncovered a plot to kidnap Aimee and hold her for ransom. Just a few months earlier a wealthy person from LA had been kidnapped and taken down to Mexico.

446 Marshall Trimble, "Aimee Semple McPherson Part II, On May 18th, 1926, Sister Aimee mysteriously disappeared off the coast of Santa Monica," *True West Magazine*, November 30, 2017, https://truewestmagazine.com/aimee-semple-mcpherson-part-ii/.

447 McPherson and Cox, *Aimee*, 164.

448 Rudd, *Aimee Semple McPherson*, 116.

449 Rudd, *Aimee Semple McPherson*, 119. An almost 90-day court case followed in which District Attorney Asa Keys, funded by local newspapers, tried to convict her and her mom Minnie on charges of criminal conspiracy. The forty-two volumes of the preliminary hearing & court case consisted of 3,500 pages. District Attorney Asa Keyes, who declared 'I know she is guilty, but I can't prove it', was later convicted of accepting bribes involved oil scandals and sentenced to the San Quentin Penitentiary.

450 McPherson and Cox, *Aimee*, 180.

451 Ibid, 197.

452 Elaine Woo, "Roberta Semple Salter, 96; daughter of L.A. evangelist," *LA Times*, February 4, 2007, http://articles.latimes.com/2007/feb/04.

453 Jack Hayford, "The Legacy of Sister Aimee: Tarnished but Triumphant," *Charisma & Christian Life*, March 1993, 16.

454 Corrie Ten Boom, *The Hiding Place*, (New York, NY: Chosen Books, 1971), 238.

455 Ten Boom, *The Hiding Place*, 114

456 Ten Boom, *The Hiding Place*, 120.

457 Corrie Ten Boom, *A Prisoner—and Yet* (London, UK: Christian Literature Crusade, 1954), 12.

458 Ibid, 13.

459 Ibid, 15.

460 Ibid, 87.

461 Ten Boom, *The Hiding Place*, 241

462 Corrie Ten Boom, *Amazing Love*, (London, UK: Christian Literature Crusade, 1954), 27.

463 Ibid, 31.

464 Ibid, 36.

465 Corrie Ten Boom and Jamie Beckingham, *Tramp for the Lord* (New York, NY: BBS Publishing Company, 1975, 1995), 185.

466 Ten Boom, *The Hiding Place*, vii.

467 Graham Williams, "Corrie Ten Boom - The Lives She Touched - video," April 23, 2017, YouTube, 1:00:41, https://www.youtube.com/watch?v=SRVDZkPnCro. Ruth Graham stated, "When I met Corrie, the thing that really impressed me was the twinkle in her eye. There was nothing but love and forgiveness."

468 Ten Boom, *The Hiding Place*, 138.

469 Ten Boom, *A Prisoner*, 129.

470 Ten Boom and Beckingham, *Tramp for the Lord*, 233.

471 Ibid, 236.

472 Ibid, 274.

473 Williams, "The Lives She Touched."

474 Ten Boom, *Amazing Love*, 10.

475 Ten Boom and Beckingham, *Tramp for the Lord*, 310.

476 David C. Downing, *The Most Reluctant Convert* (Downers Grove, IL: InterVarsity Press, 2002), 144. While younger, CS Lewis would sometimes pretend to believe and take communion, just to avoid a row with his dad; Devin Brown, *A Life Observed: A Spiritual Biography of C.S. Lewis* (Grand Rapids, MI: Brazos Press, 2013), 85.

477 Corin Scott Carnell, *Bright Shadow of Reality* (Grand Rapids, MI: William Eerdmans Publishing Company, 1974), 47. Though, to please his father, Lewis was confirmed and took his first communion, he was still a disbeliever.

478 Downing, *Reluctant Convert*, 11; Walter Hooper, ed., They Stand Together: The letters of C.S. Lewis to Arthur Greaves (1914-1963), (New York, NY: Macmillan, 1979), 135.

479 Downing, *Reluctant Convert*, 49.

480 Ibid, 51.

481 Downing, *Reluctant Convert*, 11.

482 Catherine Swift, *C.S. Lewis: Heroes of the Cross* (London, UK: Pickering and Inglish, 1989), 1, "Flora was a loving, serene yet cheerful woman."

483 Downing, *Reluctant Convert*, 33.

484 Carnell, *Bright Shadow*, 38, "Before Lewis was eight, his mother had started him in both French and Latin."

485 Terry W. Glaspey, *Not a Tame Lion: The Spiritual Legacy of CS Lewis* (Elkton, MD: Highland Books, 1996), 26.

486 Downing, *Reluctant Convert*, 35.

487 Ibid, 36.

488 Ibid, 16.

489 Ibid, 36.

490 Brown, *A Life Observed*, 48. The idolatry of education trumping family, the ignoring of the physical and sexual abuse that was too common, reminds us of many Canadian indigenous residential schools.

491 David Barratt, *C.S. Lewis and His World* (London, UK: Marshall Pickering, 1987), 5. Lewis wrote to Arthur Greeves from Malvern, "I am cooped up in this hot, ugly country of England".

492 Downing, *Reluctant Convert*, 51; Carnell, Bright Shadow, 43. Kirkpatrick intended that no pupil of his should talk 'nonsense' and he pursued every word the boy spoke, looking for inconsistencies in vocabulary, hasty generalizations, and other logical fallacies.

493 Downing, *Reluctant Convert*, 14. Downing identifies Lewis' atheism as connected with the untimely death of his mother, lasting estrangement from his father, and the relentless rationalism hammered into him by an influential mentor Kirkpatrick.

494 Ibid, 37. The Wynard school closed two years after Lewis arrived there, and Oldie (Capron) was later certified as insane; 39, Lewis wrote therapeutically about Capron in his book *The Magician's Nephew*, where he changed him from an ogre to a buffoon.

495 Ibid, 31.

496 Ibid, 30.

497 Glaspey, *Not a Tame Lion*, 30.

498 Downing, *Reluctant Convert*, 24.

499 Glaspey, *Not a Tame Lion*, 27.

500 C.S. Lewis, *Surprised By Joy* (London, UK: Butler and Tanner Ltd, 1955), 125-26, "For the whole rest of the day, whether sitting or walking, we (Jack and his dad Albert) were inseparable; and the speech (you see that it could hardly be called conversation), the speech with its cross-purposes, with its tone (inevitably) always set by him, continued intermittently till bedtime.... It was extraordinarily tiring. And in my own contributions to these talks--which were indeed too adult for me, too anecdotal, too prevailingly jocular—I was increasingly aware of an artificiality...I had to act."

501 Brown, *A Life Observed*, 7, "For much of Lewis's life, his most persistent wish when it came to God was a strong desire to be left alone."

502 Kathryn Lindskoog, *C.S. Lewis: Mere Christian* (Downers Grove, IL: Intervarsity Press, 1973, 1981), 11, regarding Albert Lewis: "He could never empty, or silence, his own mind to make room for an alien thought."

503 Swift, *Heroes of the Cross*, 1 "Albert was extremely pessimistic, irritable and prone to melodramatic outbursts."

504 Michael McCrary, "The Failure to Communicate: The Communicative Relationship Between C.S. Lewis and His Father," *Into the Wardrobe—a C.S. Lewis Website* (blog), 1994, https://cslewis.drzeus.net/papers/failure-to-communicate/, "Jack and his father had much in common."

505 Swift, *Heroes of the Cross*, 3, "Warren and Clive were given very little religious education. They were told to believe in God, to say their prayers nightly, and were regularly taken to church because 'it was the right thing to do.' But no one ever bothered to explain why."

506 Downing, *Reluctant Convert*, 84.

507 Ibid, 85.

508 Ibid, 133-34, 145. After reading George MacDonald's *Diary of an Old Soul*, he wrote Arthur Greeves on January 29, 1930, saying "one finds oneself on the main road with all humanity, and can compare notes with an endless succession of previous travelers. It is emphatically coming home"; 148, After reading William Law's book An Appeal to All that Doubt or Disbelieve, he wrote to Arthur Greeves saying, "[This is] one of those rare works which makes you say of Christianity, 'Here is the very thing you like in poetry and the romances, but this time it is true.'"

509 Carnell, *Bright Shadow*, 53.

510 Downing, *Reluctant Convert*, 148. For Lewis, Christianity would become the fountainhead of all myths and tales of enchantment, the key to all mythologies, the myth that unfolded itself in history.

511 Ibid, 135; Art Lindsley, "The Most Reluctant Convert: C.S. Lewis's Journey to Faith: A Book Review," *Knowing & Doing* (Winter 2002), https://www.cslewisinstitute.org/webfm_send/593.

512 Downing, *Reluctant Convert*, 135.

513 Downing, *Reluctant Convert*, 12, "During World War II, his *Broadcast Talks* on BBC radio made his voice the most widely recognized in Britain after that of Winston Churchill, who offered Lewis a special medal of recognition"; Perry C. Bramlett, *C.S. Lewis: Life at the Center* (Macon, GA: Peake Road, 1996), 3, "He was the most famous Christian in the world from about the middle 1940s until his death in 1963."

514 "The 50 greatest British writers since 1945," *The Times*, 5 January 2008.

515 Downing, *Reluctant Convert*, 12, 164, "the most highly regarded Christian writer of his generation"; Bramlett, *Life at the Center*, 4, "The excitement over the publication of *The Screwtape Letters* put Lewis on the cover of *Time* magazine"

516 Gerard Reed, *C.S. Lewis and the Bright Shadow of Holiness* (Beacon Hill Press, Kansas City, Kansas, 1999), 9; Angus J. L. Menuge, *CS Lewis: Lightbearer in the Shadowlands* (Crossway Books, Wheaton, Illinois, 1997), 9, Lyle Dorsett stated Lewis believed that no one would read his books five years after his death.

517 Barratt, *His World*, 44. While in prison, Charles Colson read C.S. Lewis' book *Mere Christianity*, and was struck by the intellectual and logical quality of its defense of Christianity, and by its exposure of human pride. He felt the book spoke exactly to his condition and testifies to its being an important step in his conversion. As a result of this, he founded the Prisoners' Christian Fellowship; Reed, 72, "The Oxford Prophet," *Christianity Today* (June 15, 1998); "Books of the Century," *Christianity Today* 44, no. 5 (April 24, 2000): 92. *Mere Christianity* was voted best book of the 20th century by *Christianity Today* in 2000.

518 Bramlett, *Life at the Center*, v, "The apostle to the skeptics"; David Graham, ed., *We Remember C.S. Lewis* (Nashville, TN: Broadman & Holman Publishers, 2001), 7. Dr. J.I. Packer commented, "Lewis' writing style made him seem both a fellow schoolboy and a wise old uncle simultaneously." Regarding Lewis, Packer observed that "reason plus imagination, tuned together, equals power"; Bramlett, *Life at the Center*, 3.

519 Downing, *Reluctant Convert*, 142.

520 Ibid, 143. Writing to his brother Warren in Shanghai, Jack said "In these last days, he had felt 'mere pity for the poor old chap and for the life he had led.'...The way we enjoyed

going to Little Lea (his dad's home), and the way we hated it, and the way we enjoyed hating it, as you say, one can't grasp that *that* is over."

521 Ibid, 143. In the long term, Jack became deeply ashamed about this; his father had led a lonely life, had reached out to his sons for companionship, and they had spurned him. The summer after his father's death, Jack wrote to Arthur (Greeves) that he realized that he had treated his father abominably. In 1954, the year after he was composing *Surprised by Joy*, Lewis wrote to a friend that no sin in his own life was worse than his insensitive treatment of his father.

522 "On the Wings of Eagles" (film review), Dove.org, 2017, https://dove.org/review/12605-on-wings-of-eagles/; Sally Magnusson, *The Flying Scotsman* (New York, NY: Quartet Books, Inc, 1981), 167, "The inhabitants of Weihsien were slowly starving."

523 *Chariots of Fire* took four Oscars in 1982, including best picture.

524 *On Wings of Eagles: The Eric Liddell Story*, directed by Stephen Shin and Michael Parker (2016; Culver City, CA: Sony Pictures Home Entertainment, 2017), DVD, Excerpt, "Eric Liddell—China's first gold medalist and one of Scotland's greatest athletes—returns to war-torn China," "Joseph Fiennes' *Chariots of Fire* Sequel," "He became a hero to the Chinese people, partly due to his athletic achievements—some consider him the first Chinese gold medalist"; Nigel M. Smith, "Joseph Fiennes on Chinese Sequel to *Chariots of Fire*: 'It transcends religion,'" *The Guardian*, May 15, 2016, https://www.theguardian.com/film/2016/may/15/joseph-fiennes-chariots-of-fire-sequel; Esther Laurie, "China's Hero Eric Liddell is Honored with Statue," *Church Leaders*, August 31, 2015, https://churchleaders.com/daily-buzz/261525-chinas-hero-eric-liddell-honored-statue.html.

525 Duncan Hamilton, *For the Glory* (Toronto, ON: Random House Canada, 2016), 6, 14, "The Chinese, wanting no one to forget Weihsien's woes, have created a museum… Liddell has a commemorative corner to himself."

526 Ibid, 10, "*Chariots of Fire* captures the inherent decency of Liddell."

527 John W. Keddie, *Running the Race: Eric Liddell — Olympic Champion & Missionary* (Darlington, UK: Evangelical Press, 2007), 47.

528 Magnusson, *Flying Scotsman*, 177.

529 Randy Alcorn, "The Little Known Story of Olympian Eric Liddell's Final Years," *Eternal Perspective Ministries* (blog), February 12, 2018, https://www.epm.org/blog/2018/Feb/12/olympian-eric-liddell, "My favorite lines from the movie are when Eric's character, played by actor Ian Charleson, says, 'God…made me fast. And when I run, I feel his pleasure.'"

530 Janet Benge and Geoff Benge, *Eric Liddell: Something Greater Than Gold* (Seattle, WA: YWAM Publishing, 1999), 43.

531 Benge and Benge, *Eric Liddell*, 33.

532 Diane Howard, "On Wings of Eagles: The Sequel to Chariots of Fire," *SonomaChristianHome.com*, November 2, 2017, https://sonomachristianhome.com/2017/11/on-wings-of-eagles-the-sequel-to-chariots-of-fire/.

533 Benge and Benge, *Eric Liddell*, 21-22.

534 Ibid, 34.

535 Ibid, 26.

536 Magnusson, *Flying Scotsman*, 35.

537 Ibid, 178.

538 Hamilton, *For the Glory*, 13.

539 Ibid, 13 "There was an ungainly frenzy about him. Liddell swayed, rocking like an overloaded express train, and he threw his head well back, as if studying the sky rather than the track."

540 Ibid, 42.

541 Magnusson, *Flying Scotsman*, 66.

542 Benge and Benge, *Eric Liddell*, 46; Magnusson, *Flying Scotsman*, 14.

543 Benge and Benge, *Eric Liddell*, 68. After winning in the 1924 Olympics, he was Scotland's greatest sports star; Keddie, *Running the Race*, 11, "Eric Liddell took just 47.6 seconds to

win the 400 metres race at the 1924 Paris Olympic Games… (but his victory has become a timeless moment in modern sporting history and achievement).”

544 Magnusson, *Flying Scotsman*, 12.

545 Benge and Benge, *Eric Liddell*, 72.

546 Howard, “On Wings of Eagles.”

547 David McCasland, *Eric Liddell: Pure Gold* (Oxford, UK: Lion Hudson, 2001), 295, “Florence Liddell remained in Canada where she married Murray Hall, a widower, in 1951…Eric and Flo’s three daughters, Patricia, Heather, and Maureen, have nine children among them and make their homes in Canada.”

548 Benge and Benge, *Eric Liddell*, 162, “Escorting Flo and his daughters to the ship that would take them to Canada was probably the most difficult thing Eric Liddell ever had to do in his life.”

549 Ibid, 164.

550 Ibid, 165.

551 Ibid, 167.; Hamilton, *For the Glory*, 7. The Nobel laureate Pearl S. Buck of *The Good Earth* book fame was born at Weihsien. Henry Luce, founder of *Time Magazine*, lived in the compound as a boy.

552 Ibid, 7.

553 Benge and Benge, *Eric Liddell*, 169.

554 Howard, “On Wings of Eagles.”)

555 Benge and Benge, *Eric Liddell*, 184, “[In the internment camp] Eric ran a Friday night youth group with square dancing, chess tournaments, puppet plays, and quiz shows…. Eric was probably the most popular person in the whole camp”; Eric Liddell, *The Disciplines of the Christian Life* (Nashville, TN: Abingdon Press, 1985), 15.

556 Ibid, 12.

557 Hamilton, *For the Glory*, inside cover.

558 Magnusson, *Flying Scotsman*, 180.

559 Benge and Benge, *Eric Liddell*, 163; Liddell, *Disciplines*; McCasland, *Pure Gold*, 192, “[one] of his favourite books *The Christ of the Mount* by E. Stanley Jones.”

560 Magnusson, *Flying Scotsman*, 166, “What was the secret of his consecrated life and far-reaching influence? Absolute surrender to God’s will as revealed in Jesus Christ. His was a God-controlled life”; 176, Rev. A. P. Cullen stated that, “He was literally God-controlled in his thoughts, judgement, actions, words, to an extent I have never seen surpassed, and rarely seen equalled…. First of all, absolute surrender to the will of God. Absolute surrender—those words were often on his lips, the conception was often in his mind; that God should have absolute control over every part of his life.”

561 Magnusson, *Flying Scotsman*, 165.

562 Ibid, 163.

563 Ibid, 165.

564 Ibid, 163.

565 Benge and Benge, *Eric Liddell*, 166.

566 Magnusson, *Flying Scotsman*, 162, “Most of all he was the person we turned to when personal relationships got just too impossible.”

567 Ibid, 174.

568 Hamilton, *For the Glory*, 8, “Liddell’s forbearance was remarkable. No one could ever recall a single act of envy, pettiness, hubris, or self-aggrandizement from him. He bad-mouthed nobody. He didn’t bicker…Liddell became the camp’s conscience without ever being pious, sanctimonious, or judgmental.”

569 Magnusson, *Flying Scotsman*, 163.

570 Benge and Benge, *Eric Liddell*, 198.

571 Paul Bond, “Dueling Projects to Explore What Happened After ‘Chariots of Fire,’” *Hollywood Reporter* August 17, 2015, https://www.hollywoodreporter.com/news/politics-news/dueling-projects-explore-what-happened-815567/.

572 Howard, "On Wings of Eagles," "Another fellow missionary said that Liddell's last words 'It's complete surrender' referred to his relationship with God."

573 Ibid.

574 "Eric Liddell," *Wikipedia,* June 9, 2021, https://en.wikipedia.org/wiki/Eric_Liddell,"In 1991 the University of Edinburgh erected a memorial headstone, made from Isle of Mull granite and carved by a mason in Tobermory, at the former camp site in Weifang. The simple inscription came from the Book of Isaiah 40:31: 'They shall mount up with wings as eagles; they shall run and not be weary.'"

575 Langstaff Letter, "Jesus People Movement," *Kairos Ministries,* February 11, 2016, https://kairosmin.org/2016/02/11/jesus-people-movement/.

576 Greg Laurie, "A Tribute to Pastor Chuck Smith," *Harvest.org,* October 28, 2013, https://harvest.org/resources/gregs-blog/post/a-tribute-to-pastor-chuck-smith/; lonniefrisbee-hippy, "Lonnie Frisbee and Chuck Smith," February 12, 2008, *YouTube,* 2:27, https://www.youtube.com/watch?v=JKs3aBuFhVQ, "Chuck Smith thought that we all collect-ively needed a haircut and a bath," He said, "my feeling was 'dirty hippies, why don't they take a bath?"

577 Chuck Smith and Chuck Smith Jr., *Chuck Smith Autobiography: A Memoir of Grace* (Costa Mesa, CA: Word for Today, 2009), 151, "Initially, Kay and I observed the youth migration to California with bemused fascination. These odd-looking young people seemed totally alien to American culture, yet they were our nation's sons and daughters."

578 *Frisbee: Life and Death of a Hippie Preacher,* directed by David Di Sabatino (2005; Warren, NJ: Passion River Films, 2008), Tommy Coomes commented, "Chuck Smith said to his wife Kay, 'It's too late. They are too far gone'."

579 Smith and Smith, *Memoir of Grace,* 8. Chuck Smith Jr on his mom Kay: "Mom has been Dad's partner, inspiration, and most devoted follower, sustaining him with tireless prayer support for over sixty years. Truly, the two have become one. I would hope someday that Mom would tell her story too, for it is one of great suffering, tremendous courage, and ultimate victory through the name of Jesus. She is a woman who has lived her faith in determined obedience to God—and is probably the godliest person I know"; 61-62, "More than anything, Kay was radically devoted to Jesus Christ. She embraced Him in faith as if her very existence depended on her bond with Him. Wherever He could use her, she wanted to go. Whatever path He chose for her, she wanted to follow. "

580 Ibid, 152.

581 Ibid, *157.*

582 Ibid, 158, "Within a couple of weeks, John was driving down Fairview Street in Costa Mesa when he spotted a hippie hitchhiking and noticed that he was also carrying a Bible. John pulled to the side of the road, picked him up and said, "There's someone I would like you to meet." John then drove to our home and introduced us to Lonnie Frisbee."

583 Kent Allan Philpott, *Memoirs of a Jesus Freak* (San Rafael, CA: Earthen Vessel Publishing, Kindle Edition, 2014, "Lonnie (Frisbee) was thin and below average height, with long-ish brown hair and a smattering of facial hair. He looked much like depictions of Jesus seen in art throughout the centuries. His soft, easy manner drew people. He was not a dynamic or loud preacher; he was serious yet conversational. He identified with those who had lived a hard life and were searching for answers. Lonnie loved to roam the streets of the Haight and witness to the hippies about Jesus."

584 Ibid, "At age eighteen, he moved to San Francisco with the hippies and flower children in the "Summer of Love." He described himself as a "nudist-vegetarian hippie." Lonnie did things that were highly unusual. He used to make a habit of reading scripture while on LSD. During one acid trip, he had "a vision of a vast sea of people crying out to the Lord for salvation, with (himself) in front preaching the gospel."

585 Smith and Smith, *Memoir of Grace,* 159, "We sat in our living room for several hours as he answered our questions and explained the religious and political philosophy of the hippie culture. But what we found truly fascinating was the depth of Lonnie's spiritual

perception *and insight. He constantly quoted Scripture and told us stories of what he had seen the Holy Spirit do in the lives of others."*

586 Ibid, 159, "We wanted everyone in our church to meet Lonnie. We believed that he could not only help us understand the hippies and their culture, but that his life and message could speak the truth of Jesus to them in ways we never could."

587 Neil J. Young, "The Summer of Love ended 50 years ago. It reshaped American conservatism," Vox.com, August 31, 2017, https://www.vox.com/the-big-idea/2017/8/31/16229320/ summer-of-love-jesus-people-religious-right-history, "By the summer of 1967, a half-century ago this year, nearly 100,000 hippies and counterculture kids had gathered in the Haight-Ashbury neighborhood to drop acid, indulge in free love, and escape the confining strictures of their middle-class upbringings. They wanted to join the revolution."

588 Larry Eskridge, " 'Jesus People'—a movement born from the 'Summer of Love,' " TheConversation.com,

September 15, 2017, https://theconversation.com/jesus-people-a-movement-born-from-the-summer-of-love-82421, "Drawn by nationwide publicity, somewhere between 75,000 and 100,000 youth came to Haight-Ashbury during the spring and early summer of 1967. Many became homeless, hungry and sick."

589 Philpott, *Memoirs of a Jesus Freak,* "The predators had descended into the (Haight-Ashbury) district by the middle of 1968. Even the motorcycle gangs were there in large numbers. People's minds had indeed been expanded by marijuana, LSD, peyote, magic mushrooms, and mescaline, so that heroin and meth were becoming the new drugs of choice. No one wore flowers in their hair anymore. Drug dealers were everywhere, as were the pimps and the porn makers."

590 Smith and Smith, *Memoir of Grace,* 163-164, "By the end of 1969 the optimism that characterized the early hippie movement was gone. Enough young people had either died from overdoses or permanently damaged their brains through hallucinogens that no one continued to pretend drug use was about peace and love. It was just about getting high. The curtain came down on the hippie culture in December 1969 when a young man was stabbed to death at a free concert in Altamont, California. Within two years of that event, three of the counterculture's most popular rock stars had died from overdoses."

591 Lonnie Frisbee and Roger Sachs, *Not By Might Nor By Power: The Jesus Revolution,* 2nd ed. (Santa Maria, CA: Freedom Publications, 2017), "It (The Jesus Movement) was birthed in the Haight-Ashbury, but it hit the beaches of Southern California like a spiritual tidal wave."

592 Philpott, *Memoirs of a Jesus Freak,* "The JPM was largely, but not completely, a youth movement"; Lonnie Frisbee and Roger Sachs, *Not By Might Nor By Power: The Great Commission* (Santa Maria, CA: Freedom Publications, 2016), "This well-documented Christian revival caught the attention of the whole world by 1971, and it is estimated that by 1977, ten years after this phenomenon began, two million new born-again believers came into the Christian faith. It was the largest ingathering of souls in the history of the United States, overshadowing the Great Awakenings of the eighteenth and nineteenth centuries."

593 Pastor Greg Laurie, "Chuck Smith Interview: Icons of Faith Series with Greg Laurie," October 3, 2013, YouTube, 1:10:27, https://www.youtube.com/watch?v=a64YADx_Ymk, Greg Laurie on the Jesus Movement: "It was a genuine full-blown revival"; Philpott, *Memoirs of a Jesus Freak,* "It was only in looking back at it that I realized that the JPM was an awakening like the great awakenings America had previously experienced, and this realization came primarily through reading the books of David Martin Lloyd-Jones and, above all, Iain Murray. In my book, *Awakenings in America and the Jesus People Movement,* I attempt to demonstrate that the JPM meets the requirements for inclusion in America's great awakenings"; Lonnie Frisbee, *Not By Might Nor By Power: the Jesus Revolution,* "According to statistics from Fuller Theological Seminary, the Jesus People movement was the largest ingathering of souls in the history of the United States. It overshadowed the Great Awakening."

594 Frisbee and Sachs, *The Jesus Revolution,* "(Chuck Smith) He was instantly the hippies' father figure, and you know my history with father figures. I desperately needed a good and godly role model. We all do."

595 Frisbee and Sachs, *The Jesus Revolution,* "one of my first childhood memories is of him beating my mother. As an infant, I recall him being very cruel to her, and there was a lot of screaming and crying… he traumatized me and bonded me to unnecessary brutality at a very early age. He seemed to enjoy beating his children…In fact, I don't remember ever being around my dad when he wasn't drunk…I truly hated my father ever since then. He hit me so hard in the face that I'll never forget the absolute terror and pain of that moment. It made my ears ring. I lost control of myself and went to the toilet in my pants. He was a cruel man. He bonded me to cruelty, to his violence…One time, Ray Frisbee beat my mother so badly that it closed both of her eyes until they were swollen like eggs. They turned black and blue and magenta and chartreuse. He also took a pair of broken scissors and cut all of her hair off. That was pretty much the end of that, the final blow to the marriage."

596 Ibid.

597 Smith and Smith, *Memoir of Grace,* 9, "If you had asked me in my junior year of high school what I planned to do with my life, I would have given you a ready and confident answer: 'I'm going to help people and make a decent living at the same time. I'm going to be a doctor' "; 19-20, "Still, I had no aspirations of being a minister. The thought never crossed my mind, nor do I remember a time in my youth when the ministry appealed to me. The ministers I knew were sincere, devoted men, but their lifestyle held no attraction to me. Surgeons, on the other hand, worked daily at the doorstep of life and death and had a skill that could determine on which side of the threshold their patient would land."

598 Ibid. 32. "Only one life," Harold Chalfant intoned, quoting C. T. Studd, "will soon be past; only what's done for Christ will last."

599 Pastor Greg Laurie, "Chuck Smith Interview"; Smith and Smith, *Memoir of Grace,* 39, "Like many other young people in my church, Bible reading was not a high priority for me. Instead of reading the Bible all the way through, we read select passages, generally from the Psalms and the Gospels. We also had our favorite verses that were drawn from the letters of Paul. Most of the sermons we heard were topical sermons developed from just one or two verses and supported by several other verses from different parts of the Bible. Sometimes we were given the whole context from which the verse was taken, but I cannot remember ever hearing a Bible study that took us through an entire book."

600 Ibid. 9, 47, "Secondly, I learned something about the theme of my life. It would be through my relationship with God's Word that I would leave my mark"; 83, "Not being an intellectual myself, there wasn't a danger that I would evolve into a seminarian. But standing between the intellectual giants and the average believer, I was able to translate the richness and depth of Scripture into ordinary language."

601 Pastor Greg Laurie, "Chuck Smith Interview"; Smith and Smith, *Memoir of Grace,* 88, "Simply stated, from the beginning of my ministry I had preached topical sermons, but by the time I finished the book of Romans I shifted to the expository teaching of the Bible. The transformation contained three parts: I went from preaching to teaching; the sermon went from topical to expository; and the content of the message went from my own development of a Bible text to the Bible itself."

602 Ibid. 41, "From my point of view, the spiritual life I witnessed on (Life Bible) campus had an overly emotional quality that sometimes led to impractical behavior"; 42, "The whole culture around campus and the sort of spirituality it produced felt foreign to me, which probably explains why I was the only one in my graduating class who was not "slain in the Spirit" when I received my ordination. My parents were not too pleased with my apparent lack of spirituality, nor was the college president. When I didn't go down after receiving the gentle "nudge of the Spirit" he gave me, the president leaned in close and whispered, "You'd better go down on one knee, son." The only person there who was proud of me was Kay, my lovely and devoted wife. She knew I was not a rebel, but

simply wished to be true to myself and the person God called me to be"; 44, "Given the combination of youthful idealism and chronic insecurity of eighteen- to twenty-three-year-olds, it is normal to witness a lot of posturing on Bible college campuses. LIFE had its share of super-spiritual students who let the rest of us know how frequently they retired to their rooms to pray, how many times they were slain in the Spirit, and how many hours they spent each day speaking in unknown tongues."

603 Ibid, 49, "The anointing is sometimes measured by how many wise, clever, or funny statements the preacher makes. But more often than not, the "anointed preacher" is the animated preacher who trembles and shouts. A soft-spoken preacher obviously lacks the necessary gifts to meet Pentecostal requisites. I will always appreciate my professor who urged us not to mistake perspiration for inspiration. Sadly, he spoke with quiet confidence."

604 K-Wave Radio, "Pastor Chuck Birthday Celebration—Pastors Perspective 2013-06-27," June 27, 2013, *YouTube*, 57:40, https://www.youtube.com/watch?v=W2d-DcK0FA0. Skip Heitzig, speaking about Chuck Smith, said, "He had a smile that lit up the room."

605 Smith and Smith, *Memoir of Grace*, 6, "I had barely finished the sentence when Dad said with obvious conviction, 'God prepares His vessel' "; 7, "I was silent, musing on the fact that my father obviously sees himself as defined by God's will. He then added, 'Everything is preparation for something else' "; 96, "Everything is preparation for something else. Every story is part of a larger story. Every event, regardless of whether it seems good or bad, is a seed planted, watered, sprouted, or readied for harvest."

606 Ibid, 69, "We gave it our best shot in Corona. In order to minister there and still pay our bills, I took a full-time job in a local grocery store. But nothing came easy in this season of our lives"; 73, 74, "Corona had become a disaster. In all my life I had never given up on anything. If I set out on a job or project, I always saw it through to the end. Quitting was simply not in my profile or character. But we had failed in our church, despite doing everything we knew to do, everything we had been trained to do. And now I couldn't even hold a regular job. With slumped shoulders and my head hanging down, I resigned from the church and gave up on the ministry."

607 Philpott, *Memoirs of a Jesus Freak*, "From 1968 to 1971, Frisbee made thousands of new converts with his dynamic God-Given abilities to witness to the counter-culture of hippies and surfers"; Lonnie Frisbee, *Not By Might Nor By Power: The Jesus Revolution*, "We were leading hundreds of hippies and young people to the Lord on the beaches, in our communities, in church, in Bible studies, in restaurants, at concerts, and just about everywhere. The electrifying atmosphere is so hard to capture into words. It was tangible."

608 Frisbee and Sachs, *The Jesus Movement*.

609 Smith and Smith, *Memoir of Grace*, 160, "But I think it would be more accurate to say that churches were not interested in having those 'dirty hippies' at their services, creating a distraction with the spectacle of their appearance and making church members feel nervous or uncomfortable."

610 Ibid, 167, "Word got out about "the hippie church" and people started coming just to see what all the fuss was about. Most of those who came to check out the church ended up staying."

611 Ibid, 29.

612 Frisbee and Sachs, *The Great Commission*, 96.

613 Smith and Smith, *Memoir of Grace*, 168, "One of the truly wonderful innovations of the Jesus Movement was the music. When hippies streamed into the church to worship God, they brought their own music with them."

614 Pastor Greg Laurie, "Chuck Smith Interview," "Even contemporary praise and worship began at Calvary Chapel in Costa Mesa, CA, with Chuck Smith"; Frisbee and Sachs, *The Jesus Movement*, "Contemporary Christian music was birthed in our midst. Almost overnight there were bands and musicians like Children of the Day, Love Song, Larry Norman, Barry McGuire, Andrae Crouch and the Disciples, Keith Green, 2nd Chapter of Acts, and on and on."

615 Smith and Smith, *Memoir of Grace,* 169, "Four young men who attended the Wednesday night meetings had formed a band, named Love Song, and started writing songs. One night they asked if they could sing, and when they did, the ministry of music at Calvary Chapel took a huge and historic step forward…the music of Love Song was soft rock that emphasized the harmony of their voices and considerable talent. When they sang, 'Welcome Back' for the first time before an audience, everyone was left in tears. Calvary Chapel entered a new era of music ministry. What folk music was to mass culture, rock-n-roll was to popular culture."

616 Ibid, 169, "Soon there was a proliferation of bands at Calvary Chapel and we began having weekly evangelism concerts. Other churches and Jesus People ministries up and down the West Coast heard about the bands and requested they come and play in their communities. No less than a dozen bands and single artists were touring California, performing their music and presenting the gospel in a variety of different settings."

617 Ibid, 170, "So instead, we went to the beach at Corona Del Mar, which had plenty of parking and room for a large crowd. Corona Del Mar Beach has both an area where waves roll onto the shore and a bay side that is protected by a rock jetty. We were soon baptizing hundreds and then thousands of young people every month"; Lonnie Frisbee, *Not By Might Nor By Power: the Jesus Movement,* "At one point in a two-year stretch, we were baptizing an estimated five hundred people every month, with a crowd of thousands watching and cheering and crying on the beach. It was my vision from Tahquitz Canyon being fulfilled before my very eyes."

618 Smith and Smith, *Memoir of Grace,* 171, "*Look Magazine* included a photograph of one of our beach baptisms that took up two full pages"; Philpott, *Memoirs of a Jesus Freak,* "During 1971 and 1972 the movement received extensive (and usually positive) media coverage, racking up articles in almost every newspaper in the country, even making the cover of *Time Magazine.* Nearly a hundred books celebrating, describing, and analyzing the movement made their way into print"; "He (Lonnie) was called 'the quintessential Jesus freak' and was featured in *Life* and *Time* magazines in articles documenting the "Jesus Movement" throughout North America."

619 Ibid, "One of the first Christian houses on the West Coast was Soul Inn, born out of the Lincoln Park Baptist Church. The Soul Inn began late in 1968. The House of Acts in Novato, led by Ted and Liz Wise, Dan and Sandy Sands, Jim Dopp, Steve Heathner, Lonnie Frisbee, Rick and Meagan Zacks, and others was begun earlier, sometime in 1967. It was maybe the first of all the Christian communes of the Jesus People Movement."

620 Ibid, "(CWLF) they established what became the most read publication of the JPM, *Right On.*"; Ed Hird: "I was led to Christ by the late Len Sawatsky of CWLF, attending Regent College in Vancouver, BC. As such, all the young people in our Sonlite Coffeehouse at Trinity Baptist cut their teeth on the *Right On Newspaper,* the *Letters to Street Christians* bible paraphrase, and the Spiritual Counterfeits Project."

621 Ibid, "Pat Matrisciana…produced the movie *Son Worshippers,* which was about the Jesus People Movement. In 1978, he founded Jeremiah Films." Lonnie Frisbee was prominent in the film, along with Chuck Smith, Larry Norman, and LoveSong. This film was my first step in entering the Jesus Movement in January 1972.

622 Frisbee and Sachs, *The Jesus Revolution,* "Anyway, at this particular Wednesday night service, we had *Time Magazine,* a BBC news team, and KQED 9 Public TV from the Bay Area, which later produced a documentary about the revival…*Time* did a major story on June 21, 1971, with an article titled "The New Rebel Cry: Jesus is Coming!" The cover of the magazine had a cool illustration of Jesus surrounded by the words: "The Jesus Revolution." The article covered Calvary Chapel and the massive baptisms at Corona del Mar…It became commonplace to see TV cameras, reporters, and other media people in our meetings at Calvary Chapel. Cameras were everywhere at the huge ocean baptisms at Corona del Mar…Our pictures were plastered all over the place in newspapers and then in major stories in *Time Magazine, Look,* and many other mainstream outlets."

623 Frisbee and Sachs, *The Jesus Revolution*, "I failed miserably at communicating with Connie and at meeting her needs. Like so many do in marriage, I charged forward time after time, making my bride feel perpetually in second place"; "…my wife felt isolated and left out, as my responsibilities kept me going in a million directions. It caused so much strife between us. I wrestled with conflicting priorities, usually choosing ministry over family."

624 Frisbee and Sachs, *The Great Commission*, "Then on Mother's Day 1980, Lonnie brought an anointing back from South Africa, and God poured it out on a church that met in a high school gymnasium—Calvary Chapel Yorba Linda. Another revival was eventually birthed in America, and another modern-day denomination emerged, presently called the Association of Vineyard Churches. The Vineyard presently has over a thousand churches worldwide"; 158, "I believe that I brought a move of God and an anointing back from Africa to the States and was able to help John Wimber take it around the world"; 210, "The first three or four weeks that I attended the Yorba Linda church, there were around three hundred people in a Sunday morning service. Within nine months, there were about twenty-eight hundred people coming. We had to move three times within about a two-year period!"

625 Philpott, *Memoirs of a Jesus Freak*, "Lonnie worked together with Chuck Smith and John Wimber to establish the Association of Vineyard Churches and Cavalry Chapel."; Frisbee and Sachs, *The Great Commission*, 157, "John (Wimber) eventually talked me into turning over my own ministry, World Outreach Ministries, to the Vineyard, which became the mission branch of the Vineyard. John and his board renamed it Vineyard Ministries International, or VMI. VMI has the same Federal Tax ID number as my original ministry. They only did a name change. No one really knows that, but now you do."

626 Philpott, *Memoirs of a Jesus Freak*, "I heard from people who were close to Lonnie at the time, that a kind of jealousy developed, primarily over Lonnie's notoriety, and an attempt was made to curtail the characteristic independence that Lonnie clung to. Then, after the arrival of John Wimber at Calvary Chapel, in 1970 or 1971, there was an open break, and Lonnie joined with Wimber, who had split off from Pastor Smith."

627 Frisbee and Sachs, *Set Free*, John Ruttkay commented, "At his funeral I likened him to Samson. I still do. Samson moved in God's power. Lonnie moved in God's power. Samson made choices that cost him his life. Lonnie made choices that led to his early death. But just as Samson is counted in the hall of faith, Lonnie left a legacy that continues to bring glory to God. Lonnie left behind a huge number of people who now move God's kingdom forward, and a group who continue to move in apostolic power; Marwan Bahu commented: "He was like a Samson—that guy could rip gates off of a city and haul them six miles away. Lonnie had that spiritual stature. Like each of us, he had his shortcomings, but that certainly didn't define who he was as a man of God"

628 Frisbee and Sachs, *The Great Commission*, 94, "I will say it again here: I never lived the gay lifestyle or embraced homosexuality"; 230, "As far as the allegations that I am a homosexual, I will emphatically say right here, up front that I have never lived the gay lifestyle. At the same time, I have a ton of compassion for people who have been drawn into that world. They are some of the most interesting, creative, and gifted people"; Lonnie Frisbee and Roger Sachs, *Not By Might Nor By Power: Set Free* (Santa Maria, CA: Freedom Publications, 2019), Kenn Gulliksen commented: "But for those who hear and believe rumors, Lonnie was not a homosexual. I repent over perpetuating that lie. In a so-called Christian documentary, I was asked if Lonnie was a homosexual, and answered 'yes' due to false information that I was given from some church leaders."; Some suggest that Lonnie's HIV condition came from being beat up and raped by hitchhikers.

629 Frisbee and Sachs, *The Great Commission*, 238, "After many sessions with this professional man, he told me that in all of his years as a counselor, I was the most severe case of physical, sexual, emotional, and spiritual abuse of anyone in his entire practice. He helped me tremendously to get in touch with many of the roots of my brokenness so that God could start healing me even at this late date."

630 Ibid, "The enemy of our souls tried to put bitterness, rejection, and unforgiveness on me and was doing a pretty good job. It was a tremendous battle."

631 Ibid, 148, "I do want to say again that I still love Chuck Smith. He was definitely a father figure in my life when I really needed one. He discipled and schooled me in the Word of God. How could I ever stop appreciating that? I disagreed with him in a few things over the years, but so what! I also recognize the wonderful work of all the Calvary Chapels. There are hundreds, if not thousands, of sincere and dedicated leaders as well as a multitude of believers who have found Christ and grown in their faith through the powerful work of Calvary Chapels around the world"; 175-178, "I knew there were hard feelings now between Vineyard and Calvary, which was really sad, and I wasn't trying to make it worse. I loved and still love them both. How could I not love them if I wanted to stay in tune with the Holy Spirit? I have been hurt by the Church and leaders real bad many times—but I try with all my heart to lay those things at the foot of the cross and move forward."

632 Pastor Greg Laurie, "Chuck Smith Interview," Laurie commented, "Chuck Smith is known as the father of the Jesus movement."

633 Frisbee and Sachs, *The Jesus Movement,* "We need another Jesus People Revival that will turn America and the whole world back to the true King of Kings and Lord of Lords."; Frisbee and Sachs, *Set Free,* Lou Engle in the Foreword, "A very good friend of mine recently had a dream in which he saw Lonnie Frisbee walking down the beach and heard a voice say, 'Lonnie is a friend of the Holy Spirit.' Then suddenly hundreds of literal frisbees of different shapes and sizes started flying from Lonnie all over the California beaches, up to Canada, and down to Mexico. I believe this was a prophetic glimpse of what God is getting ready to do and that we are in a new hour of the manifestation of 'Jesus the Evangelist' in the earth."

634 "John Wimber," *Vineyard USA,* 2021, https://vineyardusa.org/about/john-wimber/; KCFonline, "John Wimber's Journey Into Healing," May 22, 2016, *YouTube,* 17:29, https://www.youtube.com/watch?v=78JxKi2wTMQ.

635 Gabriel Heights Telecasting, " 'Planting and Growing Churches' by John Wimber," April 18, 2017, *YouTube,* 1:16:12, https://www.youtube.com/watch?v=SV2CBidqb-0, John Wimber was born in Kirksville, Missouri to Basil and Genevieve Estelynn (Martin) Wimber. "We live in a nation that are largely fatherless," Wimber said.

636 James J. Leutton, " 'Come, Holy Spirit': Lonnie Frisbee's Prayer and the Origins of the Vineyard Movement," M.Div. project, (2018, Malyon College, Brisbane), https://www.academia.edu/39766085/Come_Holy_Spirit_M_Div_Project_J_J_Leutton_.

637 "A brief history of the Vineyard movement," *Leeds Vineyard,* 2020, https://www.leedsvineyard.org/Articles/64918/Leeds_Vineyard/Resources/Teaching/Values_Priorities_Principles/A_brief_history.aspx, "His band, the Righteous Brothers, had two albums in the top ten—but his marriage was falling apart."

638 Gabriel Heights Telecasting, " 'Planting and Growing Churches' by John Wimber."

639 KCFonline, "John Wimber | The Cost of Commitment," August 25, 2018, *YouTube,* 1:07:40, https://www.youtube.com/watch?v=tELD7kvcLug.

640 Gainesville Vineyard, "The Memorial Service of John Wimber Nov. 21, 1997," June 15, 2020, *YouTube,* 2:43:41, https://www.youtube.com/watch?v=17n5l31wm9Y. John Wimber would say, "All I was trying to do is read the book and obey it"; "Again and again I was being taught fundamental obedience."

641 KCFonline, "The Cost of Commitment."

642 New Life City, "Tim Wimber: May 6, 2017 | Word & Power Session 6," May 9, 2017, *YouTube,* 1:21:09, https://youtu.be/1_2TTWjBgho, "[John Wimber] was a salesman for a collection agency."

643 inthelight1776, "John Wimber Vineyard Signs & Wonders Conf 1985 10/12," January 30, 2013, *YouTube* [no longer available], https://www.youtube.com/watch?v=2NfM3TVxjNs, Dr. Don Williams said, "He kind of looks a little like Santa Claus. Don't you...? He's kind of a guy that you just want to jump on his lap and tell him what you want for

Christmas"; John Dart and Bonnie Hayes, "Renowned Pastor Wimber Dies at 63," *Los Angeles Times,* November 18, 1997, https://www.latimes.com/archives/la-xpm-1997-nov-18-me-55098-story.html, "Wimber, who was said to resemble a cross between Kenny Rogers and Santa Claus.")

644 Friendsbehindtrees, "Lonnie Frisbee—Mother's Day 1980 Full Sermon," November 15, 2016, *YouTube,* 1:07:54, https://www.youtube.com/watch?v=2ylugDXtStw, on John Wimber: "He kinda reminds me of a Teddy Bear."

645 Sam Storms, " 'Doin' the Stuff (Remembering John Wimber)," *SamStorms.org,* 2021, https://www.samstorms.org/all-articles/post/doin-the-stuff---remembering-john-wimber--, "But don't be misled by John's humor. One should never mistake his simplicity for simple-mindedness. He often referred to himself as "just a fat man trying to get to heaven," but he was extremely well-read and theologically discerning. I don't know if I've ever met anyone as street wise as John or as perceptive of the dynamics of human nature."

646 Gabriel Heights Telecasting," "John Wimber's Vision," April 14, 2017, *YouTube,* 1:30:52, https://www.youtube.com/watch?v=C2eHp2VY4M4.

647 Jane Skjoldli, " 'God is Blowing Everybody's Mind': Three Controversies that Helped Shape the Vineyard Movement," *Alternative Spirituality and Religion Review* 4, no. 2 (2013), https://www.academia.edu/39184438/_God_is_Blowing_Everybodys_Mind_Three_Controversies_that_Helped_Shape_the_Vineyard_Movement "From 1974 to 1977, Wimber was a church growth consultant at the Fuller Theological Seminary, under C. Peter Wagner."

648 Donald Kammer, "The Perplexing Power of John Wimber's Power Encounters," *Churchman* 106, no. 1 (1992), https://churchsociety.org/docs/churchman/106/Cman_106_1_Kammer.pdf.

649 Leutton, "Come Holy Spirit," "By 1976, Wimber had moved his church out of its Quaker association as a result of his acceptance and use of the spiritual gift of tongues, and had found a home with the Calvary Chapel movement."

650 "John Wimber," Vineyard USA.

651 Skjoldli, "God is Blowing," "If any charisma was particularly important to Wimber, it was healing. He began to pray for healing in his services, calling people with various illnesses to come forward and accept prayer on their behalf. For months, their prayers seemed in vain. Then, one morning in 1978, Wimber prayed for a woman with a high fever. To his and the woman's husband's surprise, she got well. Wimber 'stumbled out the door, jubilation suddenly filled him and he shouted, 'We got one!'"

652 "John Wimber," Vineyard USA; Lawrence Sit, "A Comparison Between the Views on the Work of the Holy Spirit of John Wesley and John Wimber," MA term paper (2017, Chinese University of Hong Kong), https://www.academia.edu/36494201/A_comparison_between_the_view_of_the_work_of_Holy_Spirit_of_John_Wesley_and_John_Wimber, "Similarly, the value of experience is the driving principle for the Wimberism 'everyone gets to play,' a modification of the reformation value 'the priesthood of all believers' to include the empowerment of all believers."

653 Dart and Hayes, "Renowned Pastor Wimber Dies at 63"; Storms, "Doin' the Stuff.")

654 Inthelight1776, "John Wimber Vineyard Signs & Wonders Conf 1985 10/12," "If you're going to encourage your church to learn to minister (in the area of healing ministry), you have to give them room to fail, and you have to give them permission to fail...My posture is 'It's okay to blow it.' I am going to love whether you blow it or not. The only thing I get uptight about is a bad attitude, if I have someone who has a sinful attitude, someone who is real proud, or someone who won't take counsel. I can put up with a lot of things."

655 Ibid, "Don't put on airs. Don't be mystical. Don't try to put on spiritual mannerisms. Be genuine. Be honest. Then you can maintain some integrity. Once you start cheating the system and act spiritual, you've ended all chance of being spiritually effective, because the only person you are cheating the most is yourself."

656 Gainesville Vineyard, "Memorial Service," Bob Fulton said, "The reason I can follow John is that he knows how to repent. And when people tell him this is wrong and he sees it, he is easy to repent...In John, there wasn't any hype...He never tried to hype... to wind a crowd up"; "He wasn't looking for the approval of people."

657 Storms, "Doin' the Stuff," "John may well have been the most overly analyzed and criticized man in America during the 80's and early 90's. But he refused to retaliate in kind. He was gentle, but strong, kind, yet forceful when needed, always humble and self-effacing but not afraid to express his opinions or wield his authority when he believed it important to do so."

658 KCFonline, "Cost of Commitment," "Becoming a disciple is committing yourself to being uncomfortable the rest of your life. Becoming a disciple is committing yourself to being a learner the rest of your life. Becoming a disciple is committing yourself to risk-taking the rest of your life, just always having to take chances"; "Faith is spelled 'R.I.S.K.'"

659 Skjoldli, "God is Blowing," Ft. 243, "None of us had a clue as to what was going to happen next. When they got to the front the speaker said, 'For years now the Holy Spirit has been grieved by the church, but he's getting over it. Come, Holy Spirit.' And he came.... One fellow, Tim, started bouncing. His arms flung out and he fell over, but one of his hands accidentally hit a mike stand and he took it down with him. He was tangled up in the cord with the mike next to his mouth. Then he began speaking in tongues, so the sound went throughout the gymnasium.... Carol Wimber also reported that previous occurrences like this had been few: 'We had seen a few people tremble and fall over before and we had seen many healings, but this was different. The majority of young people were shaking and falling over. At one point, it looked like a battlefield scene'."

660 Ibid, "For (Chuck) Smith, casting demons out of Christians was the final straw; immunity from possession was supposed to be one of the privileges of being saved. Already uneasy with the multiplication of Spirit manifestations that demanded increasing amounts of attention during services, exorcism appears to have been the deal breaker for Smith and likeminded Calvary Chapel leaders."

661 Leutton, "Come Holy Spirit."

662 "John Wimber," Vineyard USA. https://vineyardusa.org/about/john-wimber/; Leutton, "Come Holy Spirit."

663 Leutton, "Come Holy Spirit."

664 Dean Krueger, "John Wimber - Kingdom of God," July 21, 2016, *YouTube*, 1:28:04, https://www.youtube.com/watch?v=3u84U64MEFo.

665 Stephen Hunt, "The Anglican Wimberites," *Pneuma* 17, no. 1 (Spr 1995), https://www.deepdyve.com/lp/brill/the-anglican-wimberites-UyRSl2Urta: 106, "One of the most significant connections that grew out of this period was the relationship between Wimber and the Anglican church in Britain. Sandy Miller, vicar of Holy Trinity Brompton (HTB), said Wimber "had a greater impact on the Church of England than anyone since John Wesley"; Sit, "A Comparison," "Don Williams cites Anglican Bishop David Pytches as suggesting that Wimber was the 'greatest impact on the Church of England since John Wesley.'"

666 Thomas Lyons, "Authorities for Discernment: The Wesleyan Quadrilateral in the Ministry of John Wimber" (2013, Society of Vineyard Scholars), https://www.academia.edu/40140195/Authorities_For_Discernment_The_Wesleyan_Quadrilateral_in_the_Ministry_of_John_Wimber, "[A] brief conversation with Bob Fulton at the 2011 Vineyard National Convention revealed that John Wimber used to read Wesley's journals as part of his devotions because Wimber said he felt a great kinship with Wesley"; Ft 11, "Bob Fulton, Personal Interview. 03 May, 2011...When the Spirit was poured out on Mother's Day, 1980 during the ministry time of Lonnie Frisbee, Wimber looked to Wesley (and Whitefield) for precedent."

667 Vineyard Churches UK & Ireland, "Legacy // An interview with Carol Wimber, Penny Fulton and Bob Fulton," April 11, 2020, *YouTube*, 54:25, https://www.youtube.com/

watch?v=97dOO3vlFJc. Bob Fulton stated: "John considered David Pytches the bravest man he had ever known, because he took a lot of heat for what had happened. Carol Wimber: We all considered David Pytches our man in the UK."

668 KCFonline, "Memorial Service," Carol Wimber said: "John loved the whole Church… he didn't think of the Vineyard as any more than one vegetable in the whole stew…He didn't think that we were it.")

669 Leutton, "Come Holy Spirit"; Kammer, "Perplexing Power."

670 Alister McGrath, *J.I. Packer: A Biography* (Grand Rapids, MI: Baker Books, 1997), 1.

671 Leland Ryken, *J.I. Packer: An Evangelical Life* (Wheaton, IL: Crossway, 2015), 23.

672 Ibid, 24, In a Christianity Today polling of their contributors of the ten best religious books of the twentieth century, Packer chose the Lord of the Rings trilogy by JRR Tolkien, saying "a classic for children from 9 to 90. Bears constant rereading"; 30, Packer said that at age 17, he became 'a Dostoyevsky addict', much impressed by how the Russian novelist 'takes the skin off his characters and allows us to see what they are like.'

673 McGrath, *Packer*, 11 "He was a solitary figure, who found greatest pleasure in reading and studying."; Ryken, *Packer*, 21, "From his early years, Packer was a shy boy who did not mingle easily with his peers."

674 Ibid, 23.

675 McGrath, *Packer*, 3, 45 "His parents were poor, and he had no private means."; Ryken, 20. "…J.I. Packer came from humble roots. …he has never lost his common touch."

676 McGrath, *Packer*, 9.

677 Ryken, *Packer*, 29.

678 Timothy George, ed., *J.I. Packer and the Evangelical Future: The Impact of His Life and Thought* (Grand Rapids, MI: Baker Academic, 2009), 10, "It was in meetings of the Oxford Inter-Collegiate Christian Union, a British version of Inter Varsity, that Packer found a living relationship with Jesus Christ and committed his life to Christian service."

679 Ryken, *Packer*, 39.

680 George, *Evangelical Future*, 25. J.I. Packer, "The Comfort of Conservatism," in Power Religion, ed. M. Horton (Chicago, IL: Moody, 1992), 288; George, *Evangelical Future*, 20, McGrath commented: "Packer's distinctive and, in my view, critically important insight that evangelical theology is both enriched and stabilized by attentiveness to the past"; George, *Evangelical Future*, 26, McGrath commented, "Packer argues that attentiveness to the past liberates us from 'chronological snobbery' and alerts us to the riches of past readings of Scripture."

681 McGrath, *Packer*, 43, "Packer mentioned that he was a Puritan addict"; 55, Packer commented, "Without Owen, I might well have gone off my head or gotten boggled down in mystical fanaticism"; 77, "the Keswick teaching had come to be seen as a distinctive article of evangelicalism. To criticize Keswick was thus to attack evangelicalism."

682 Ibid, 54.

683 Ibid, 22, 24, 25, 26, "The discovery of Owens must be regarded as marking a turning point in Packer's Christian life"; 43, "Packer explained that John Owen's sixty pages on mortifying sin had helped him cope with 'popular brand of holiness teaching, which was driving [him] around the bend' "; 56, "What do the Puritans have to offer modern evangelicalism? The answer for Packer can be summed up in a single word -maturity."

684 Ibid, 46, "Packer's growing interest in the theology of the Puritans had led him to explore the writings of Richard Baxter (1615-91)"; 47, "Packer's thesis The Redemption and Restoration of Man in the Thought of Richard Baxter was long; its 499 pages extend to nearly 150,000 words. (Oxford would later insist that doctoral theses should not exceed 100,000 words.) The work shows Packer as a scholar with a gift for rigorous analysis and clarity of expression."

685 Neil Bramble, "J.I. Packer," *Convivium*, May 12, 2017, https://www.convivium.ca/voices/124_j_i_packer/, "The essence of Puritanism is not the public caricature often imposed upon them, but a lively, sincere, and devoted spirituality based on the Bible's teachings translated into one's personal life."

686 McGrath, *Packer,* 179, "one of the twentieth century's most influential and admired Christian books *–Knowing God*"; 256, "Packer's bestseller *Knowing God* represented a classic statement and justification of the intimate relationship between knowing correct ideas about God and the relational activity of knowing God."

687 Ibid, xi, "James Innell Packer is one of the best-known names in modern Christianity."

688 Ibid, xi, "…one such person who has made a major long-term contribution to the shaping of Christianity in the modern world."; George, *Evangelical Future,* back cover, "J.I. Packer is one of the most significant evangelical theologians of the last one hundred years." (Timothy George is the Executive Editor for *Christianity Today*.)

689 Ibid, 20.

690 McGrath, *Packer,* 290.

691 George, *Evangelical Future,* 10.

692 J.I. Packer, *Knowing God Study Guide* (Madison, WI: Intervarsity Press, 1975), 7, "Packer…wrote *Knowing God* from the conviction that ignorance of God lies at the root of the contemporary church's weakness."

693 Warren Cole Smith, "Patriarch—Dr. J.I. Packer," *Virtue Online,* December 1, 2009, https://virtueonline.org/patriarch-dr-j-i-packer, "The *(Knowing God)* book, first published in 1973 and now translated into at least seven languages, has sold more than 2 million copies, an astounding number for what is essentially a textbook in basic theology. "It was a surprise," he told me: "I wrote the first draft as a series of articles. It was essentially intended as a catechesis—a teaching book. At first I just hoped that it would go into a second printing."

694 McGrath, *Packer,* 191, McGrath commented that …this was the right book for the right moment.

695 Ibid, 191.; Ryken, *Packer,* 114, "Indeed, Stott and Packer were the two most prominent evangelical leaders in the Church of England during the 1960s and 1970s."

696 McGrath, *Packer,* 195.

697 Ibid, 62, 161, "Packer had been one of the relatively few evangelicals of influence within the Church of England who had championed links with Lloyd-Jones."

698 Ibid, 157 "Lloyd-Jones…wrote to Packer to terminate the Puritan Conferences" in the context of the 1970 publication of the *Growing into Union* book by two evangelicals and two Anglo-Catholics. It was renamed the *Westminster Conferences.*

699 Ibid, 53.

700 Martyn Lloyd-Jones, *Revival* (Crossway Books, Wheaton, Illinois, USA, 1987), foreword.

701 J.I. Packer, "Marks of Revival," *Grace Online Library,* 1998, http://graceonlinelibrary.org/church-ministry/revival/marks-of-revival-by-j-i-packer/. Awareness of God's presence. The first and fundamental feature in revival is the sense that God has drawn awesomely near in his holiness, mercy, and might.

702 J.I. Packer, "The Glory of God and the Reviving of Religion," 100-104, in Justin Taylor, "What Is Revival?" *The Gospel Coalition,* February 17, 2010, " 'Revival is God touching minds and hearts in an arresting, devastating, exalting way, to draw them to himself through working from the inside out rather than from the outside in. It is God accelerating, intensifying, and extending the work of grace that goes on in every Christian's life, but is sometimes overshadowed and somewhat smothered by the impact of other forces. It is the near presence of God giving new power to the gospel of sin and grace. It is the Holy Spirit sensitizing souls to divine realities and so generating deep-level responses to God in the form of faith and repentance, praise and prayer, love and joy, works of benevolence and service and initiatives of outreach and sharing.' What is the pattern of genuine revival? Packer suggests the following ten elements:
"God comes down.
God's Word pierces.
Man's sin is seen.
Christ's cross is valued.
Change goes deep.

Love breaks out.

Joy fills hearts.

Each church becomes itself—becomes, that is, the people of the divine presence in an experiential, as distinct from merely notional, sense.

The lost are found.

Satan keeps pace."

703 McGrath, *Packer,* 180, "In the eyes of many young evangelicals, Packer and Moyter together (at Trinity College, Bristol) represented a form of evangelicalism which possessed both intellectual rigour and spiritual integrity," 237.

704 Ibid, 181, "As Trinity settled down, Packer again found he had time and space for thinking, speaking, and writing.… Packer was able to negotiate an arrangement with the college Council, by which he would spend the autumn and spring terms teaching in Bristol, leaving the summer term free of commitments in order to allow him to spend time in North America.… Increasingly, Packer became a well-known figure in North America—not simply through his books, but through his personal presence at seminaries as a teacher and lecturer."

705 Ibid, 233; Bramble, *Packer,* "Packer could have had a number of other teaching positions in high profile seminaries in the United States, but he chose the fledgling Regent College, where 37 years later (2016) he is still involved—in his ninety-first year."

706 McGrath, *Packer,* 217, "Packer was by now regarded in North America as the best-known and most highly respected British evangelical theologian. …His book *Knowing God* had firmly established him as one of the most important writers in the area of spirituality… In short, Packer was being lionized in North America. In England, however, he was being marginalized."; Ryken, *Packer,* 165, "Mark Noll notes that the British posts (temporary teaching assignments) were Anglican; the North American posts have been Reformed and evangelical."

707 Ibid, 164.

708 McGrath, *Packer,* 239. "By the end of the 1980s, Regent was the largest graduate institution of theological education in the region with a new purpose-built home on a high-profile site on the university campus."

709 Charles Colson, "Packer, Puritans and Postmoderns," in ed. Timothy George, *J.I. Packer and the Evangelical Future: The Impact of His Life and Thought* (Grand Rapids, MI: Baker Academic, 2009), 139.

710 McGrath, *Packer,* 160, "Two major events of the 1990s—the Anglican Church of Canada's Essentials '94 congress…can be seen to rest on precisely the theological foundations developed by Packer in England during the 1970s…it represented the application of a coherent and historically and theologically justified approach, which had been set in place twenty years earlier"; 283, "Packer…was the chief architect of 'Essentials 94.'"

711 George, *Evangelical Future,* 11 "Packer has been ever mindful of the maxim of Richard Baxter, on whom he wrote his Oxford doctoral dissertation. In *necessariis Unitas,* in *non-necessariis Libertas,* in *utrisque Caritas*"; 12, "Packer is by nature a peacemaker and a gentle man, yet he has had a career of controversy…his stand on religious issues has often made him an object of criticism."

712 George, *Evangelical Future,* 10.

713 Bramble, *Packer,* "The term collaborator may well describe Packer's most telling leadership quality. He loved working as a member of a team, and he did so on numerous occasions. Perhaps the best example was his role as general editor in producing the English Standard Version of the Bible. Interestingly, Packer himself sees this as his most significant contribution."

714 TS4M, "J.I. Packer—On Personal Holiness," March 6, 2014, *YouTube,* 51:29, https://www.youtube.com/watch?v=EDnk-jSz7Z4: When I was eighteen years ago, I spoke to a conference "For the rest of my working life, I should be conducting a crusade for catechesis, that is, the revival of catechism type instruction in all evangelical churches. What is the essence of catechetical instruction? It is two things together, teaching the doctrines

of the bible, teaching the truths that we are to live by, and teaching in direct connect with that, how to live by those truths, how to practice in fact what we called holiness." "I want to campaign for a renewal of personal holiness…" "…culturally the West is coming apart…" "we don't make as much of repentance as we should."

715 J.I. Packer, *Marks of Revival*, Revival Commentary, v. 1, n. 1, in "Page for May 30," Your Father Loves You (Wheaton, IL: Harold Shaw Publishing, 1986): "Revival is the visitation of God which brings to life Christians who have been sleeping and restores a deep sense of God's near presence and holiness. Thence springs a vivid sense of sin and a profound exercise of heart in repentance, praise, and love, with an evangelistic outflow." Source: *Your Father Loves You*, Shaw Publishing, 1986, Page for May 30.)

716 McGrath, *Packer*, ix, "my Christian calling thus far has felt so much like me 'and a few other blokes' trying to stop specific falsehoods, nail specific sins, and further the new life that Satan tries to quench in his ongoing war with the God of creation, providence, and grace."

717 J.I. Packer, "Revival #2," *SermonAudio.com*, February 18, 2004, https://www.sermonaudio.com/sermoninfo.asp?SID=2190484710, A Southern Baptist conference at Grenville Seminary, South Carolina, USA: 3:33, "In revival, God comes close, and thus sin is seen, and because sin is seen, the gospel is loved, as never before, and repentance goes deep, and godliness grows fast, and the church becomes itself, and the world feels the impact as an evangelistic overflow, and Satan keeps pace trying to spoil and corrupt what is going on." 24:50, "Dr Lloyd-Jones hoped for revival until he died. He is gone. The prophets are gone, but we should still be hoping for revival. Revival is a sovereign work of God. He fixes the time table. The schedule is his, not ours. 49:43, "Revival means the overcoming of hostile spiritual forces, forces against which the people of God have thus far been impotent, forces which have run all over them, forces of secularity, forces of worldliness. There is always opposition when revival begins, and regularly there is opposition to the gospel before revival begins." "And have you studied the East African revival of our own time? It broke in the 1930s. It's still going on. It dies down and flairs up again like a forest fire…It prepared the people of God…for the appalling convulsions that they had to go through politically and in terms of persecution…The revival folks stood firm under persecution when the Mau-mau folk were trying to get them back to the tribal darkness of ethnic, witch doctor-type polytheism. They wouldn't go. Many of them lost their lives at the time…If God hadn't quickened his people by revival blessing in the 1930s and thereafter, where would the Church be in East Africa?" 1:04:35 paraphrase: Revival is a rediscovery of the blessing (the central revival doctrine) of justification (by faith). 1:0513, Revival is…the people of God pictured as a candle stick sustained and enabled to burn and burn and keep on burning through oil from heaven… revival means power, constant sustained power from God's Holy Spirit for life and service; 1:09:29 Revival means the purging out of sin from the lives of saint through bringing them to repentance. (sins vomited up); 1:18:38, Revival shows God to be still on his throne, victorious…a demonstration of his sovereign Lordship and sovereign grace.

J.I. Packer, "Revival #3," *SermonAudio.com*, February 19, 2004, https://www.sermonaudio.com/sermoninfo.asp?SID=2190484748, 16:11, A Southern Baptist conference at Grenville Seminary, South Carolina, USA: "The alternatives are always revival or judgement, and that is as true for us in North America today as it was in the Bible times." 19:43, "God is sovereign in revival. You cannot predict it, but also you cannot preclude it. There is no situation so grave and so grievous that God cannot move in it and restore it." 20:15, "Spiritual revival is something to be sought, to be sought for one's own soul, to be sought for one's own church, to be sought for one's own community. It is not for us to say all we can do is wait and twiddle our thumbs until God is pleased to act." "We are to seek spiritual renewal, spiritual revival, and we are to seek it by petition…linked with self-examination." 24:20, "Spiritual revival is something to be sought for and looked for. God does not play cat and mouse with us." 25:00, "Pessimism about the possibility of revival is a form of unbelief of the Bible."

We would like to thank our good friend Bill Glasgow of Wm. Glasgow Design in Abbotsford, BC for his creative book design, Larry Luby our publisher with His Publishing Group in Dallas, Texas, and Gordie Stackhouse for his back-cover photo. We give honour and glory to God for giving us the encouragement and stamina to write this book at this difficult period of time on the Earth.

CPSIA information can be obtained
at www.ICGtesting.com
Printed in the USA
BVHW061257031221
622841BV00002B/13